Unlock Your Personalization

Unlock Your Personalization
Ramjee Prasad

AALBORG **UNIVERSITY PRESS** • 2012

To Society

Everyone owes a debt to society. To repay it, I have decided to serve it by dispensing the C5 concept to help bring peace and serenity to humanity.

Left: The ambition to create happiness and pleasure in society
Reference - Knud Erik Færgemann:
thography, Aalborg University)

Content

Preface	9
Acknowledgements	13
1 - Introduction	15
1.1 Personalization	17
1.2 Successful cases	21
1.3 Life's Stages	23
1.4 Correlation - life phase and C5	27
1.5 A stress and tension-free life and nights of peaceful sleep	27
1.6 Mind and its infinite energy	27
1.7 Steering the mind in the simplest way	29
2 - The basics of C5	31
2.1 Introduction	31
2.2 The five W's	34
2.3 Creativity	35

2.4 Contentment	36
2.5 Confidence	37
2.6 Calmness	39
2.7 Concentration	40
2.8 C5 Practice	41
2.8.1 Practicing C5	43
2.8.2 Daily routine	44

3 - A Reality — 47
3.1 Introduction	48
3.2 Learning process	49
3.3 First series of sessions in 2004	51
3.4 Second series of sessions in 2005	60
3.5 The impact and results of Leo's activities and experiences with C5	63
3.6 Conclusions and recommendations	65

4 - A Truth — 67
4.1 Inga's background	67
4.2 Thoughts about goals	69
4.3 C5 Practicing	70
4.4 Impact factor	71

5 - Toward Quality of Life (QoL) — 75
5.1 Quality of Life (QoL)	76
5.2 Making C5 happen	78
5.3 A dream toward reality and truth	80
5.4 Unlocking the personalization	80

Author — 83

> **Openness** of mind is a gateway toward **creating** a **global** village

Preface

Unlock Your Personalization is a unique book that offers a simple way of learning to steer and control your mind toward happiness and success. It explains the five basic elements of human life, namely Concentration, Calmness, Confidence, Contentment and Creativity as illustrated here as C5.

I conceived the C5 concept in 1962 when I was 16. Since then I have been practicing it in my daily life and I have advised several people to do the same to help free them from stress and tension, and enable them to enjoy restful nights of sleep. Two successful case stories illustrate the strength of the concept: Leo from the Netherlands and Inga from Denmark. They are introduced in Chapters 3 and 4, respectively.

Managing stress requires a clear understanding of your mental state. You need to understand how to unlock your

hidden mental potential. You should always remember that you are much stronger than you imagine. The likely reason why some people do not believe in their own great strength of mind is that they have neither discovered nor used it. Like most things in life, the mind atrophies with the lack of use. This hidden potential will never be realized as long as its existence is not known and experienced. Often, people do not realize the potential of their minds but keep it locked up through stress, tension and a lack of sleep, a situation that can eventually lead to a severe mental block. A locked mind is unable to generate creative and innovative ideas. All this leads to what I call locked personalization.

A series of steps that unlock the mind are described in the C5 concept. C5 provides the foundation for living a richly creative and successful life with no-stress, no-tension and sound sleep; in other words it leads to quality of life (QoL) in the real sense of the word. The C5 concept should not be confused with yoga, as this combines exercise with meditation. The C5 concept can be practiced by anyone, young or old. Starting at a young age enables you to realize the concept in the truest sense by practicing it throughout your life.

The contents of the book are illustrated by the figure. The book itself is the outcome of my personal experiences and the experiences of several other people who have profited from applying C5, particularly those of Leo and Inga already mentioned above. The idea for writing this book came when I saw how successfully Inga and Leo had been applying the C5 concept. I realized that there is a need for the C5 concept to help everyone achieve a peaceful life. C5 will bring peace and serenity to individuals, to society and to countries as a whole, and it will make the world a better place to live in. To the best of my knowledge, this is the first book of its kind. It explains in a simple way how to steer and control your mind to achieve your personalization goals.

ft: Illustration of successful C5 of Leo
eference - Johs. Hofmeister:
tract of Lithography, Aalborg University)

Illustration of successful C5 of Inga
(Reference - Bjørn Nordahl:
"Seated woman", sculpture, 1990,
Aalborg University)

C5 A Paragon

5 - Towards Quality of Life

4 - A Truth

3 - A Reality

2 - C5 Concept

1 - Introduction

Unlock your Personalization

(Photo: colourbox.com.)

Coverage of the book

Chapter 1 explains the meaning of personalization discusses life's divisions and explains how to steer the mind in order to utilize its infinite energy, at the same time ensuring you have a stress-free, tension-free life with nights full of sleep. The basic concept of C5 is explained in Chapter 2. It gives a description of the individual elements of C5, namely Creativity, Contentment, Confidence, Calmness, and Concentration and discusses how to put them into practice.

Chapter 3 presents a real-life case story from the Netherlands, as experienced by Leo. He presents his experiences and his successful use of C5 in real life. In Chapter 4, I lay out the strong evidence supporting the truth of C5. This chapter also presents Inga's case from Denmark. She is of the opinion that C5 will bring about change that will lead to a peaceful society.

Chapter 5 concludes the book by introducing the Quality of Life (QoL) concept. This chapter also discusses how C5 can be disseminated to the broader world.

The completion of this book gives me the same pleasure as I imagine a gardener feels on seeing his garden in full bloom. The book is an introduction to the C5 concept. In due course, more books will follow. The present book provides the basics of the C5 concept so that everyone can start practicing. I hope it will help you create a new life, free of stress and tension and with restful nights.

Acknowledgements

I would like to express my heartfelt thanks to Leo and Inga, without whom this book would never have been written. Both have motivated and encouraged me to express my ideas in this book, to the benefit of society. In particular, my thanks go to Finn Kjærsdam, President of Aalborg University, for his early support of this project. I greatly appreciate the help provided by Junko, Alice, Kirti, Vrinda, Adam, Morten, Mayuri, Albena, Pernille and Kirsten. Last, but not least, I would like to thank my family - my wife, Jyoti, and my children, Neeli, Anand and Rajeev, as well as my lovely grandchildren, Sneha, Ruchika, Akash and Arya – for their continuous and unconditional support.

Chapter 1

> There is **enormous** **capacity** within every human being that should be properly utilized to **achieve** your goals

Introduction

From my wide experience, I have come to realize that everywhere in the world people face enormous problems stemming from heavy workloads, stress and anxiety. In our post-modern, techno-science era every effort is being made to achieve a good standard of living for people. "Globalization", "multinational capitalism", or "consumer capitalism" play important roles and have become key words in everyday life. To increase their chances of finding jobs, education, housing, and transportation, the majority of people are moving away from rural areas to the metropolitan centers. There they are expected to succeed in innovative, challenging, competitive jobs involving the meeting of a constant succession of deadlines.

Researchers, engineers, doctors and other academicians hold jobs which are even more challenging and demanding than in the past. Stress can be the outcome of such a challenging career. On the one hand, taking up the challenge and entering the competition is the road to success. A successful person believes that he/she is a winner and thus feels happy. But in the attempt to achieve success you turn into a workaholic and become tense; and the fear of failure can lead to even greater tension. Having to accomplish tasks within time limits adds to the stress. At the same time, you have to keep your personal and social life in balance. At some point you feel that you are not achieving the results you expected from your job. You feel you are a failure and start thinking that everything is out of control. This leads to further stress and then anxiety sets in.

This is already a major problem in the western world and, as a result of the economic conditions and competition for too few jobs, developing countries are now facing the same problem.

In this era of communication technology, all kinds of information are at our fingertips and this adds to mankind's intellectual burden. In a manner of speaking, the world is becoming smaller; within minutes new information can be spread to every corner of the globe. This development is going to escalate and everyone needs to learn to cope with the rapid changes in life style because they provoke stress.

The various factors which contribute to creating stress are called stressors and they cause negative emotions like tension, anxiety, frustration, etc. Stressors affecting family life include changes in your relationships. They can be financial problems resulting from such changes. At work, the pressure to perform can develop into work-related stress. The stress caused by having to constantly adjust to new technologies is the newest type of stress and is a growing factor in our times. The young generation is strongly affected by such developments. Social stressors, change stressors, decision stressors, and physical stressors – these are some other common types of stressors that are prevalent in modern society. The fact is that some of these stress-related situations are inevitable. But the intensity and duration of the stress can vary depending upon a person's nature and situation. In an ideal world, you could turn your back on stressful situations, or change them. But in practice, this is rarely possible.

Prolonged periods of emotional stress result in a build-up of tension that may cause physical, physiological and psychological distress. Stress is related to a number of complaints, such as sleep disturbances, headaches, fatigue, muscle tension, back or neck problems, stomach distress, frequent colds and infections, rapid breathing, a pounding heartbeat, high blood pressure, and trembling. The victims of stress may also suffer from anxiety, irritability, fear and embarrassment. They may find it hard to concentrate and make decisions and they experience repetitive thoughts, self-criticism, forgetfulness and restlessness. Short-term effects include sleeplessness and changes in eating habits; in the long term the result may be a crisis which affects the person's physical health and family relationships. It is therefore very important to relieve a state of stress as soon as possible.

Typically, people suffering from prolonged stress consult their doctor for help. Some people try to relax by watching TV or listening to music. They take a walk, play games or use medication. These all are positive things. But some start smoking or take to drink – as a result they could lose control of the situation. These methods of relaxation only treat the symptoms and give no real relief. After some time, the tiredness and stress will return and grow worse because the strength and potential of the person's mind, body and intellect have not been stimulated. A more powerful solution for the problem is needed. It is possible to learn to control your response to these situations and develop techniques that will reduce the effects of stress on mental and physical health.

It is my view that the C5 technique can give your mind and body the rest it needs and help you explore the full potential of your mind. This in turn will improve the strength of your body and increase the quality of your work – this is the path toward personal development. To create something extraordinary or achieve something special, you need a determination driven by a body and mind running at their full potential. Under stressful conditions, it is very difficult to fully utilize one's potential. Only a healthy body and a happy mind can yield a 100 % output.

Quality of life (QoL) concerns not only people's wealth and employment, but also their physical environment, physical and mental health, education, recreation and leisure time, and social life. Our materialistic lifestyle with stress, tension and sleepless nights makes us unhappy – this is not the good life.

Working as a scientist and a professor, I have developed and explored the quality of services that utilize the potentials of new communication technology. I have now turned to developing the C5 technique to improve QoL, i.e., a life free of stress, tension and sleeping problems. This is the gateway to personalization.

I have dedicated a large part of my life to the evolution of the C5 concept. When I was 16, the seeds of C5 started to grow in my mind. As a young student in India, I taught C5 to senior persons such as advocates and judges from all over the country. They were tense and stressed due to the demands of their work. At that time I used to discuss their problems in the natural environment. I addressed the importance of concentration and confidence to them. It proved to be beneficial in solving their problems. Practicing C5 made them stress-free and tension-free. After that I left India to share my knowledge globally. I continued practicing C5 every day and I still practice regularly. In my professional life many students and professors have come to me with their problems. I have tried to solve their professional as well as their personal problems concerning family life and stress. This experience with people and the knowledge and awareness has helped me to develop and explore C5 further. All of this has served as a basis for assisting mankind.

Reflections on the Book

Life can indeed be enjoyable. To make this come true you need a real visualization. This is what this book will teach you.

The management of your daily life is a key issue. Although achieving an understanding of 'daily life management' at an early age is optimal, it is never too late to start – better late than never.

The development starts with a basic understanding of "personalization", followed by "life's stages", explaining "mind", its infinite energy, and how to steer it in the simplest way. Two successful examples are then discussed.

1.1 Personalization

"Personalization" is a key word in human daily life. It can be interpreted as your unique recognition of your own efforts and the means at your disposal for your own achievement or creation. You have the ability to achieve something special. Achieving it may lead to personal success and full satisfaction in life. This is what personalization is all about. Due to your unique creativity, you should come forward with something new that can constitute your individual personality. Personalization is the creativity or essential character that makes up your identity.

Your creativity will be different from that of all others, making you special – one of a kind. Personalization is the pursuit of personal achievement. It is the process of personal development through your determination and will power. Determination and self-discipline enable you to build your personalization despite the difficulties you meet. You were given your family name by birth but personalization is achieved by using your own strengths and results in the creation of your unique identity.

Creativity is the process of inventing or introducing something new – something that had not been noticed or perceived by others. Everybody had watched an apple fall, but it took Isaac Newton to formulate the law of gravity. Your creativity comes through your own effort.

Whether an artist, engineer, doctor, administrator, actor, social worker, politician, etc., you can aim to create a novel objective/goal that will earn you recognition locally, regionally, or globally. There are many ways to do this, for example by changing or modifying something in a way that demonstrates that it obviously originated or belonged to you. Anything that the mind can conceive is achievable. The image illustrates the road to success. You become a successful person by virtue of your distinctive character or qualities. Your personality is your own creation.

Humility is the most important quality for someone to reach their objective/goal of personalization. Being humble means being without pride and arrogance. Humility, or humbleness, reflects the quality of being courteously respectful to others. It is the opposite of aggressiveness, arrogance, boastfulness, and vanity. Rather than "Me first", humility allows us to say, "No, you first, my friend." Humility is the quality that lets us go more than halfway to meet the needs and demands of others. A question

Right: A successful person
(Model Photo: colourbox.com.)

that comes up all the time is, "does being humble lower one's esteem?" The answer is no. A humble person never thinks of being the brightest, cleverest, strongest, best looking person in the world.

A humble person ultimately prospers and wins more respect than a person who is proud and powerful. Humility has no regard for possession or accomplishment. There is no need to advertise anything. What success it brings is taken as a natural gift.

The meaning of humility is well explained by the help of the tree. The magnificent tree is full of fruits. As they ripen, the branches of the tree will bend. Its sweet fruits are meant for all the creatures in the world. The modest tree selflessly serves life on earth with its fruits but still bends with humility.

The important thing to remember is that "nothing fails like success". The more successful you become the more humble, grateful and devoted you should be. Like the fruitful tree, you should share your knowledge, experience and the fruits of your success with all mankind. If, at the peak of success, you stop making the effort that brought you to the top of the mountain this will be the very moment you begin sliding down into the valley.

Everyone is trying to achieve personalization and create a personal network to make a successful life. In this modern world everybody is moving

A humble tree (Photo: colourbox.com.)

along the personalization path, but unfortunately, many have no success. The result is stress, tension and sleepless nights. Worries and problems flitting around in your mind continually make you feel as if there was a heavy weight holding you down. Sometimes, these mental problems build up slowly and you are not even aware of how much you are struggling to carry this burden around.

Stress triggers can be external or internal. Internal triggers can arise from your own mind, anxiety and your nature. External stress comes from society, the environment, the family and ill luck. Though you are perfect in your own work, people like to point out shortcomings. Such instances form the major source of societal stress. Different people will be affected in different ways by any particular event.

Therefore the causes of stress should be eliminated and finally society has to be transformed so that everybody enjoys a life free of stress, tension and sleeping problems. Only this will unlock your personalization.

The new C5 concept of concentration, calmness, confidence, contentment and creativity will make this transformation happen. The C5 concept is a successful method for opening the window for utilizing the infinite strength of mind and body. Everyone can reach his/her objective to enjoy QoL.

1.2 Successful cases

I taught the C5 technique to many advocates and judges when I was studying at Birla Institute of Technology (BIT) in India. Practicing C5 brought them success in their lives, both personally and professionally. It was never my intention to introduce the C5 concept to the general public because I have always had a very busy schedule, working 16 to 18 hours every day on my scientific and educational activities. However, the following two success stories have encouraged me to make the benefits of C5 known to a wider public.

Leo is a professor in the Netherlands and director of a very big research center in the field of telecommunications. In order to handle his extreme workload I advised Leo to practice the C5 concept. He found it so beneficial that he decided to contribute to the writing of Chapter 3 in this book, and he will also join me in establishing a center for C5. Chapter 3 presents in detail Leo's personal experience and his opinion about C5.

Inga from Denmark expressed her willingness to learn C5 in 2008. She started practicing it and within a short time she felt the value of C5 in her daily life. She also decided to participate in C5 activities and she has written Chapter 4.

After Leo's and Inga's success with C5 I realized the importance of the concept for human life and felt that it was my duty to contribute to making the world a happier and more creative place to live in. This is what motivated me to write this book so that people are given the opportunity to understand the C5 concept. I discussed my strategy and vision for introducing C5 to the general public with Leo and Inga. I wanted to open center first in Denmark, then in the Netherlands and later elsewhere. Both Leo and Inga showed their interest in establishing the center and gave their full support.

In order to get a better grasp of the idea, it is important to understand how life changes with age. This is explained in the following sections.

1.3 Life's Stages

As I see it, life is divided into five stages, namely,

i) Innocence,
ii) Intelligence,
iii) Innovativeness,
iv) Involvement, and
v) Infinity

Life has several milestones, marked both by continuity and variation. Every milestone is characterized by its specific process, that is, "generating", "operating" and "destructing evils". The whole process is nothing but "G (generation), O (operation) and D (destruction)".

The understanding of the three terms generation, operation and destruction express the fact of life. The 5 stages of life is made accordingly. Age is a very important factor. It has been given very thorough consideration in the process of defining the stages of life: Innocence (up to 5 years of age), Intelligence (5-25 years), Innovativeness (25-50 years), Involvement (50-75 years), and Infinity (above 75 years).

1.3.1 Innocence

"Innocence" covers the period up to the age of five. This is the age of childhood when children are at their most innocent. This stage should be the best part of your life, when you enjoy life to the full. You are unaware of the real world, so you are living in your own merry universe. Sorrow has no part in your life – it is only later that you come to know the harsh realities of a life which requires you to be able to survive.

1.3.2 Intelligence

"Intelligence" designates life from the age of 5 to 25. It is the age when you go to school, college and university to gain knowledge and wisdom. You learn new things every day and become more intelligent as you grow, you learn about more and more new issues. You see the real world, full of complexity. You learn how to cope with problems; it is the time when you become more and more aware of reality. As you become aware of reality, you have to bear more and more responsibilities and you are put under ever increasing pressure. This phase also brings emotional awareness to your life. It does not mean that you have been emotionally unaware until then, only that you can now direct and refine those emotions.

The age from 18 to 25 can be categorized as the age of youth and intelligence. In this phase of life, human beings have an incredible and enormous potential to make positive contributions not only to their own nation but also to the world as a whole.

1.3.3 Innovativeness

Education does not end with graduation from formal schooling. The first 25 years are meant to equip human beings with essential tools to be used in the next phase of life. The innovative part of life is the age between 25 to 50 years. It is the age when you apply

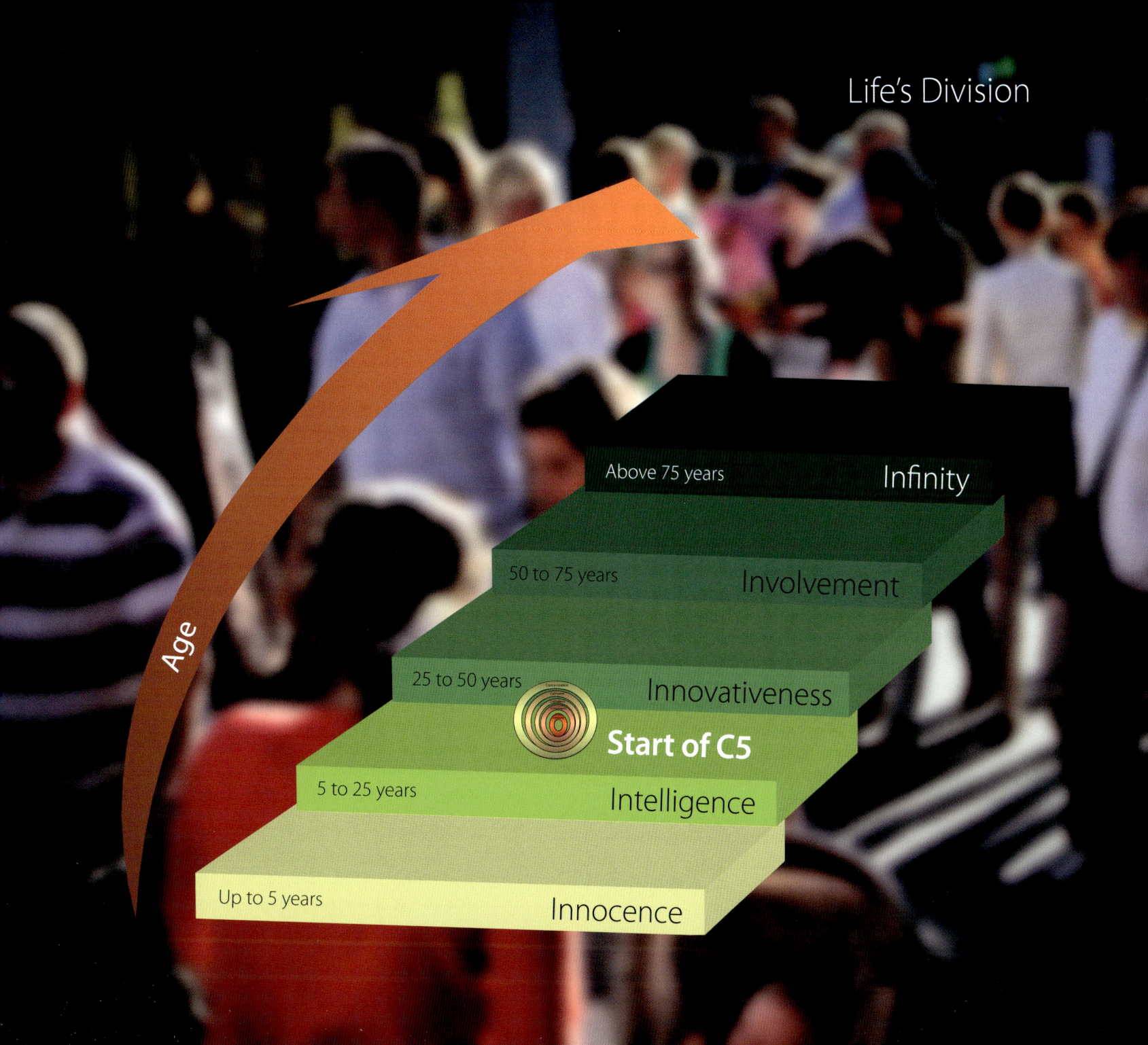

the intelligence gained during the "Intelligent" period of life. It is really the time to be creative to reach certain goals. You must define the goals to be achieved. The sky is the limit. An aimless mind is like a rudderless ship at sea. Defining the aim is one thing, but to achieve it requires effort.

There are several approaches to being successful in your endeavors. Making a continuous effort is one of them. The question below makes it clearer.

Standing at the foot of the mountain of innovation and **gazing** upward, how can you **climb** it, if you **never** try?

The heights reached by great individuals as a result of a long struggle require continuous efforts and cannot be attained by a sudden flight – while their companions were sleeping, they were struggling upward.

Tired is a meaningless word. If you work happily to reach the goal, you will never feel tired.

Every effort you make brings results that increase your creativity. Whatever the result is, you should be contented. Contentment is the finest thing in the world. You should always have confidence in yourself, be full of calmness, and remain concentrated on reaching your aim. Creativity, contentment, confidence, calmness and concentration (C5) are among the highest human virtues and they form the foundation of human life. The concept of C5 is established during this phase of life. A detailed explanation is given in Chapter 2.

1.3.4 Involvement
The "Involvement" part of life is the age between 50 and 75 years. After the period of creativity, you should be fully involved with people and with society as a whole. You should share your experience with everybody. It is the age when you are very active again but in a different way. This time of life is more about concentrating on sharing your achieved wisdom with others, as opposed to sharing your practical knowledge, which is often obsolete by this stage anyway.

A human being is a social animal by nature. This helps society move forward in accordance with the D5 circle (Direction, determination, depht, decision and Duration). The right direction is to be full of determination and to use the in-depth knowledge you generated during the innovative part of your life. The next important factors are decision-making and defining the duration.

1.3.5 Infinity
The "Infinite" part of life is the age between 75 and infinity. Although its length is indefinite, the only given thing in human life is its END. So this is the period when you should offer lessons for people in other stages of life. You should be

D5 elements

full of happiness when you reach the end. The circle of life starts with the innocence phase and, in reality, it also ends with innocence. It is nothing but a point in time. So why have stress? Why be tense? This is also a period during which people seek to prepare themselves for passing life's "final examination". It is ideally a time for meditation and contemplation on the eternal verities.

1.4 Correlation - life phase and C5

The seed of C5 practice should be sown in the intelligence phase. Your ability to concentrate, to focus on your personal goals, will determine that you have a successful and happy life and succeed in contributing to society as a whole. This is the starting point of the journey of personalization. The conscious decision to maximize your creativity will define the direction of your life.

In the innovation phase, as you make a concerted effort and determine the depths of your knowledge, you can organize your mind and achieve creativity. You will gain in confidence when you experience the positive consequences of your success and creativity. In this phase you can develop your creativity with full confidence and concentration.

As you move toward the involvement phase with experience and maturity, you become neutral and start looking at your achievements with calmness. You share your wisdom and knowledge with those around you. In this phase you are involved in action that is beneficial for society.

You can feel pride and contentment about your accomplishments when you reach the last phase. The END of life should be filled with contentment about your efforts, wisdom, creativity, and the results you gained.

1.5 A stress and tension-free life and nights of peaceful sleep

Dividing life into five stages and describing how the stages should be filled in, does not mean that in reality society is confronted with strong deviations. A very large population lives with stress and tension. In fact, this is the most common cause of ill health in our society.

The challenge is how to turn the tables so that stress will affect fewer people. "Is this possible?" you may ask. Yes, it is possible. Most of the stress that we live with is self-generated, and as we have caused it ourselves, we can do something about it.

Never say no to any challenge. The C5 concept will make it possible. You need to practice C5 every day – it takes so little to make life happy and successful.

The basic concept of C5 and how to practice is explained in Chapter 2.

1.6 Mind and its infinite energy

The human mind and the body are two-in-one. Together they can lead us along the path of success. The only point that needs to be recognized is that the mind and the body are full of energy and you should learn how to utilize this energy toward the successful path. The human mind harbors ideas. Those thoughts are not isolated events; they contain energy and can influence reality. The energy generated by the human mind is released into the world and shapes your destiny. The C5 concept makes it happen.

The human mind processes enough energy for you to reach your goal of personalization. It is only a matter of how it is utilized. Its utilization fully depends on how seriously the C5 is practiced in daily life and on steering the mind in a right direction. This is briefly discussed in next section.

1.7 Steering the mind in the simplest way

The speed of light is nothing compared to that of the mind. At one moment, your mind is in Washington and in the next, it is in Tokyo. So controlling the mind properly is truly a big challenge. Concentration offers a simple way of steering your mind. You must remain focused on your objective. Being focused means centering attention on something such as a goal or a problem. Once you start focusing and concentrating fully on the issue at hand your mind will remain in Washington so long as it is required. Learning to focus drastically increases your potential for success in your chosen career. Focusing along with the right attitude can create wonders. The image shows a focused person.

Right: Mind steeri
(Reference- Poul Anker Bech: "Preoccupation", extract of painting, 199
Aalborg Universit

The C5 Concept

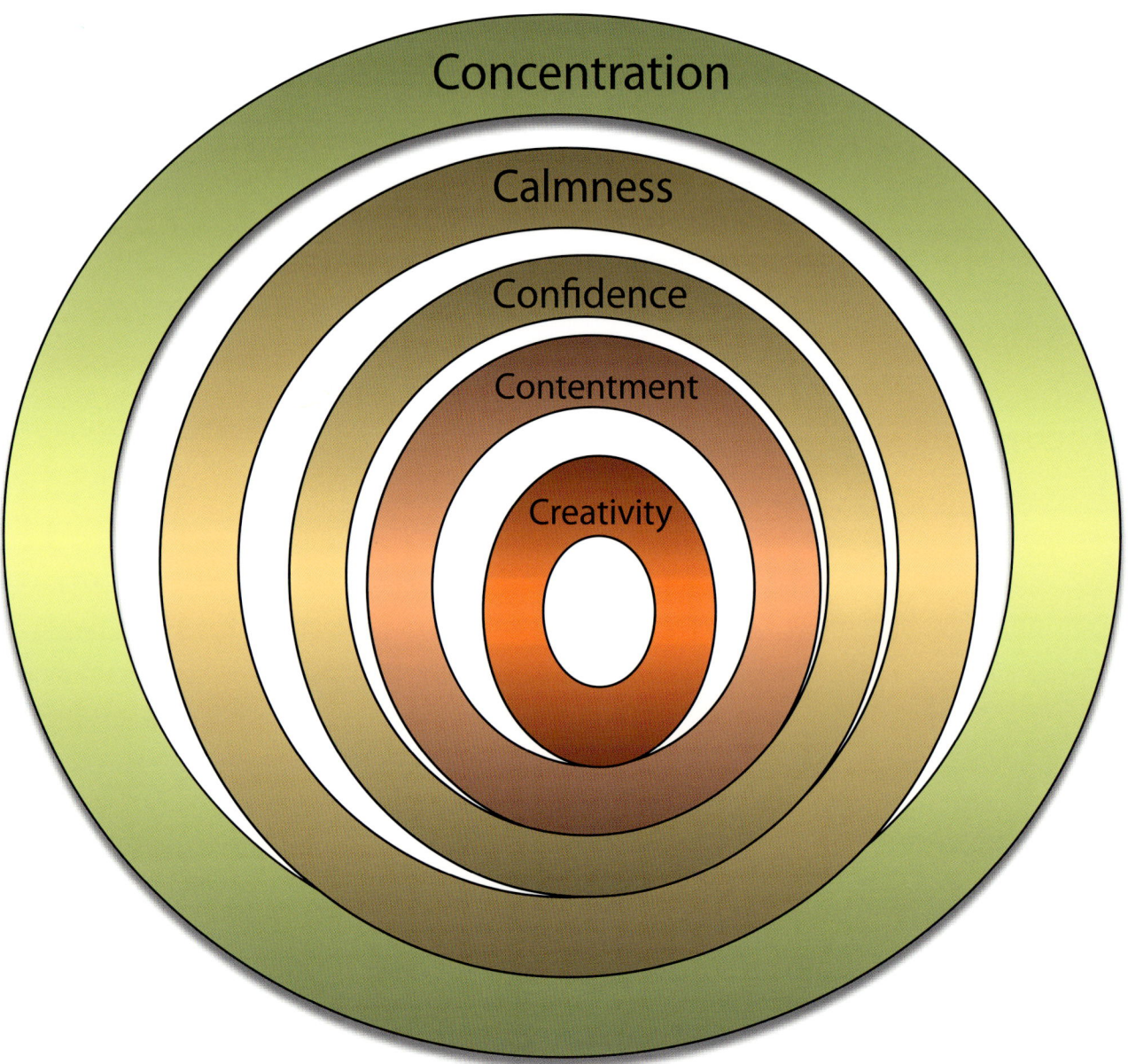

Chapter 2

> *When 'Mind' and 'Body' are joined together, any **positive** vision and mission **can be achieved***

The basics of C5

2.1 Introduction

C5 stands for Concentration, Calmness, Confidence, Contentment and Creativity, as illustrated in the figure.

I conceived the C5 concept in July 1962 when I was 16 years old. It was during the school summer holidays and I was staying with my mother in Babhnaur (72 km from Bodh Gaya) to plan my future education. Mother and my elder brother wanted to send me to one of the top engineering colleges in India in accordance with my late father's desire for me to become a top engineering student. At first, I had disagreed with my family. I wanted to study fundamental physics and then join the Fundamental Research Laboratory to do basic scientific research.

There was an outside room in our village home where I used to sit and think about my future career in science. It was very quiet and my desk was near a window. One hot sunny afternoon I was fully absorbed in my thoughts, observing the landscape outside and listening to the music of the birds singing. Suddenly, I decided to go out with my pen and paper and walk around in the countryside. I kept on walking for hours and hours, sometimes sitting down to note down my thoughts. Finally, I stopped when it had got completely dark and I found myself in a village far away from my home, thirsty and hungry. I had walked almost continuously for about six hours. I stayed the night in the village with a family known to my father. Early next morning I left and reached home at about 13.00 hrs. I had been away for almost for 24 hours. When I got back I could see that my mother was seriously worried about me. She was in tears, but then I made her happy by telling her that I would study engineering.

On the path leading to C5 enlightenment
(Reference - Gerda Andrea: "After rain, Sønderho, Fanø",
pastel picture, 1990. Aalborg University)

During the 24 hours I spent alone, I did some serious thinking about the choices I should make for my future life. While walking for those many hours I thought and thought. I thought in great depth. I realized that my family was a very important part of my life. My decision to study fundamental physics would shatter their dream to see me as an engineer. I thought that if I developed creativity in my life, I could also do research as an engineer. This is how the first C - creativity - of the C5 concept took form. The process of thinking deeply happened because I was fully concentrated on my thoughts. Concentration became my second C. My self-confidence led me to choose the right things in my career path. Confidence forms the third C. At the age of 16 I defined only 3C's. I developed the further two important C's, calmness and contentment, as I made my journey through life. In short this is the story of the birth of the C5 concept. C5 led me to choose engineering as my career.

Babhnaur village, where I was born, is very near to Bodh Gaya. Bodh Gaya is famous for being the place where Gautama Buddha attained Enlightenment. I used to go to this sacred place very often to sit under the tree there and spend a lot of time thinking. Bodh Gaya inspired me and has always been a source of positive energy.

In 1963 I was admitted to the Bihar Institute of Technology, now known as the Birsa Institute of Technology, or BIT. BIT is in the heavily industrialized town of Sindri. I decided to study telecommunications and BIT was the leading technical institute in Bihar at the time. During my five years of study I continued to develop the C5 concept by practicing it properly and also by discussing it with the people, mostly senior engineers, working in local industries. During my studies I had the opportunity to give lessons on C5 to many prominent people such as lawyers and judges. These people had successful careers, status and money – yet they were not happy. I explained the importance of calmness and confidence to them. I used to give the C5 lessons in a very calm and peaceful environment, away from the daily hustle and bustle of the city. The judges used to share their problems with me and I used to teach them how to practice the 5C's.

My village home
(Reference - Gerda Andrea: "The garden of Peter Seeberg",
pastel picture, 1990. Aalborg University)

My happy family

Then I moved to Ranchi for further study at Birla Institute of Technology in 1968. There I met Jyoti and we got married in 1969.

I completed my Master and PhD degrees in Plasma Physics and continued practicing and giving lessons on C5 till 1983. During my stay in Ranchi, we were blessed with our three children, Neeli in 1970, Anand 1972, and Rajeev in 1976.

Practicing C5 has given me a happy family and, with Jyoti's support, it gave me the strength to grow personally, family-wise, and professionally. In 1983, I moved to the University of Dar-es-Salaam in Tanzania, then in 1988 to Delft University of Technology in the Netherlands, and finally, in 1999, to Aalborg University in Denmark. During this period my children completed their education, got married, and now I am the grandfather of four. C5 continued to be the foundation of my happy family life as well as the development of my personalization. This was a period of tremendous growth with over sixty PhD students, 25 books published, and a lot of other things going on. Among several of the foundations I helped to start, the Center for Wireless Personal Communication in 1997 in Delft and the Center for TeleInFrastruktur (CTIF) at Aalborg University in 2004 are worth mentioning. As a result of my long practice of C5, and experience of sharing it with several other people, my conclusion is that the practice of C5 provides a good basis not only for living a stress-free and tension-free life with nights of peaceful sleep, but also for a happy family life.

After this brief introduction, Chapter 2 is organized as follows. Sections 2.2 and 2.3 explain creativity and contentment. Confidence is described in section 2.4, calmness in section 2.5 and concentration in section 2.6. Section 2.7 is wholly devoted to the practice of C5 in daily life, independently or with a partner.

2.2 The five W's
C5 is a phenomenon of utmost importance in our lives. Therefore, we should nurture it with our full abilities. It should be focused from the starting point of its definition by asking, "What?", "Who?", "Whom?", "When?", "Where?" (W5).

What is the deeper meaning of W5? W5 is a way of gaining a clear understanding of C5, i.e., Concentration, Calmness, Confidence, Contentment and Creativity.

The answers to all five W5 questions in relation to C5 can be summed up in one sentence: C5 is a fundamental theory for human life that applies to everyone and it can be practiced at any time and place.

2.3 Creativity
Creativity is the most basic element of the C5 concept. Creativity refers to the ability whereby a person creates something new that has some kind of value. It may be a product, a solution, a work of art, and many other things. You should be creative at every stage in life. To be creative, you must have a dream with a definite goal. Making your dream become reality requires an enormous effort.

What is creativity?
Creativity is a realistic goal. What is involved varies from person to person, from time to time and from one part of life to another. It is extremely important to unlock your creativity to fulfill your personalization but your full determination is required.

Who is creative?
This is a surprising question and its answer is also a surprise. Every human being is creative in some way or an-

other. It is important to have a clear understanding of this, because otherwise you may go in the wrong direction.

Creativity starts in childhood so the parents play a very significant role in making their children creative. Parents should sow the seed of creativity by motivating their children.

Every individual is creative but its objectives may change from one stage of life to the next.

To whom is creativity related?
Everyone has his/her own creativity, but it has an effect on society as a whole. It also depends on the objective. Every objective begins and ends with personalization.

So, you should be careful when defining the objective and scope of your creativity. Although it is fully connected with personalization, society also plays a role.

When is the right time to initiate creativity?
Creativity should be stimulated from early in life. Its goal can be short-term, long-term or even life-long. Creativity is a continuous process that changes with time. Time is the most important factor in human life. Time and the tide wait for no-one. Time is the most important gift endowed by the GOD.

Opportunity is like courting a capricious lover; you have to be in the right place at the right time. Opportunity is a giant-like feature with long hair in front and oily (slippery) with no hair in the back. You should catch the opportunity at the right time from the front, with long hair; otherwise you will slip at the back that is oily. If you are

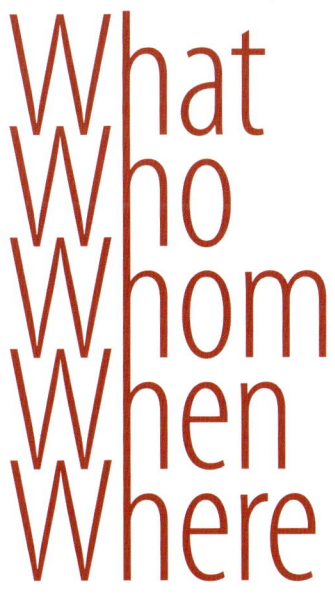

not able to catch an opportunity in a fraction of a moment, you miss it.

Where is creativity initiated?
It should be initiated whenever the opportunity arises. When and where are interrelated points. Opportunity can come at any time and in any place, the thing is to recognize it and be ready to catch it.

2.4 Contentment

Contentment follows creativity. Contentment means being satisfied with your lot. It is happiness which brings tranquility. It is good to be creative and it is important to be content with whatever you achieve.

People are creative, but not everybody achieves their goals. People should be satisfied with what they achieve. Otherwise, they will become stressed, tense and get sleeping problems. But you can overcome this, if you learn to be content. Therefore, contentment is the finest thing in the world. Those who learn to be content are the most motivated to become successful in life. Contentment is nothing but the sportsman spirit. Do everything that you want to do, and if you do not get the desired result, try again and again. In the end, you will definitely achieve your goal.

"Failures are the pillars of success". The path to success is not an even one. It is like a very steep hill; reaching the highest point can be tough. Failures are inevitable on the road to success. Instead of viewing failure as something to be avoided you should turn it into a "stepping stone" on the path to success and gratification. In other words: Success is the destination, whereas failure is how you get there.

The behavior of spiders is a very good illustration of how to achieve success. They try to climb a wall. They try once, and then fall down; they keep on trying again and again till they succeed. The way spiders climb walls gives you a very important lesson in life. Sometimes it takes years or even longer to achieve your envisioned goal. Very few people make it at their first attempt, and many, not even on their second, third, fourth or fifth attempts. So how long should you keep going before giving up? It depends on how much you believe in your dreams and goals, and wanting them enough to battle for them. It depends on your determination and perseverance. Ultimately, it depends on never losing sight of what you want to achieve. You have to treat every setback as another learning experience rather than as another defeat, such as spiders do while climbing walls.

Just as W5 is related to creativity, it is also related to contentment. Here are some questions and answers about W5 with reference to contentment.

What is contentment?
Contentment is to be happy, to be satisfied irrespective of the result. It is the point where the mind needs to be controlled.

Who is content?
You need to be content and after experiencing failure you should try again and again. Contentment is the key to success.

Contentment is related to whom?
Contentment is related to you, your family, your friends, and so on. The results affect family and friends. So, your happiness radiates happiness out into your environment.

When should you be content?
Life should be ruled by the simple philosophy that work is done for its own sake and that you should keep your mind busy for the next step. There should not be a pause because you reach one goal; it should be a continuous process. So, the answer is, every moment should be full of happiness and contentment.

Where is contentment to be found?
Everywhere is the place for contentment, whether you are in the playground, in the classroom, in the office, and so on.

2.5 Confidence
Confidence is the essential point for the C5, both from its placement as number three and its value.

Confidence makes everything happen on the road to achieving personalization. Confidence is nothing but your will to keep on going toward your goal. Confidence governs the mind and steers it in the right direction so as to utilize its infinite energy and make everything happen! Confidence means the belief in your ability to succeed. The key element in self-confidence is, therefore, an acceptance of the many consequences of a particular situation, whether they are good or bad. When you do not dwell on negative consequences you can be more 'self-confident' because you worry far less about failure or the disagreement of others following a potential failure. You are then more likely to focus on the situation at hand, which means that enjoyment and success also become probable. Confidence comes when you believe in your ability to perform an activity and this comes through successful experience. For example, you need self-confidence to speak in front of a group of people. You have to look and feel confident when faced with the challenge of giving a presentation or a speech to a large audience. If you feel confident it will be reflected in the reaction you get from the audience which in turn boosts your confidence and spurs you on to success.

The other four elements of C5, namely "concentration", "calmness", "contentment" and "creativity", depend to a large extent on the essential element "confidence". So, if you are fully confident, you can initiate your creativity, you will always be content, and without any doubt you will find calmness and your mind will be fully concentrated.

Confidence comes automatically because of the infinite energy of the mind. There is no idea that cannot be achieved if it is properly conceived. It may happen in the second attempt, the third attempt, and so on - but it will happen.

The W5 questions are what?, who?, whom?, when? where?, and here are the answers with reference to "confidence":

What is confidence?
Confidence is having the will-power to achieve creativity toward personalization.

Who should feel confidence?
Who should not be confident? Creativity has to be achieved via the infinite energy of the mind. The point is only to steer it in the right direction. Confidence makes it happen.

In whom can confidence be built up?
Questions 2 and 3 are interrelated. They are both subjective issues. It is in everybody.

When should confidence be established?
It has to be established right from the beginning in the concept phase of creativity. It will help in defining creativity properly.

Where is confidence located?
Confidence is at the heart of all creativity. It is the right location and keeps the mind and body together to run the whole operation successfully. For a confident person, the sky is the limit.

2.6 Calmness
Calmness helps you achieve success. Calmness brings peace to your family, to your environment, and to everyone. Calmness is the real source of peace in the world.

Calmness increases strength in order that you can reach your goal. You should remain calm at all times and places. It is significant for realizing any dream.

In your sleep you can dream of being at the top. The same dream can be realized in real life if you are calm in the stressful situations you face while trying to achieve the dream.

The question is how to go about retaining one's calmness. The answer lies in another question: why can you not remain calm?

A series of questions can be raised in answering this question. The real answer is, everyone must remain calm to make life wonderful. It is the point of realization – the point of happening – the point of everything!

Calmness is related to W5 just like creativity, contentment and confidence. Again, a series of questions and answers provides the answers.

What is calmness?
Calmness is a state of mind that keeps you balanced when you are making decisions, working, having a conversation, participating in meetings, and so on. Calmness is really special feature!

Who should be in a state of calmness?
To bring peace to the world everyone should be in a state of calmness. Calmness is not only a sign of success; it is also a sign of a peaceful world. How good it would be if everyone were to become calm.

For whom is calmness significant?
Calmness is significant for anyone in any situation. Calmness is the mental state of being free from agitation, excitement, or disturbance. We can learn from nature to be calm as in the image. Calmness creates a peaceful working environment.

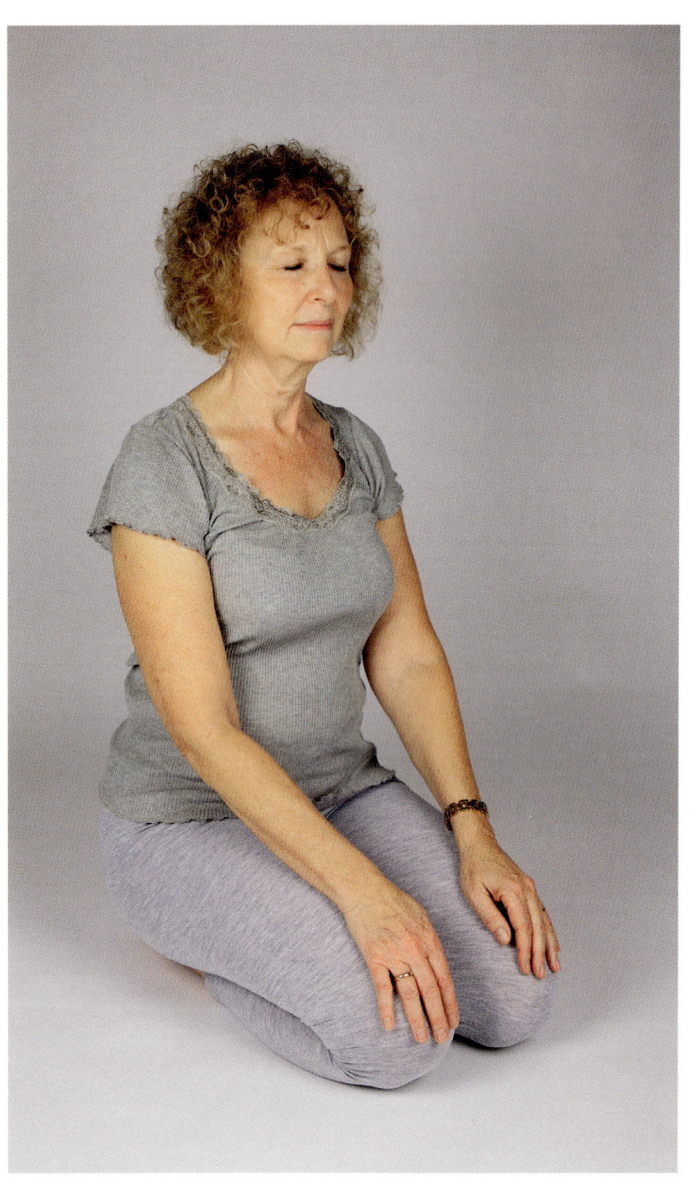

Concentration
Concentration requires a good posture, as in the image

When is calmness required?
When is calmness not required? The answer is simple and takes the form of a question, but it is well thought out.

Where is calmness necessary?
As in connection with "when", the question is – where is calmness not necessary?

2.7 Concentration
Concentration is the first and the last position in the C5 concept, depending on whether you use a top-down or a bottom-up approach. In both cases, it is significant. If the first applies, it must be carefully thought through; if the latter; it is the gateway to success. The same is true for the location of creativity. Both have their own purpose and meaning.

However, concentration is the medium that leads to successful creativity.

Concentration means focusing on one and one thing only; this is the objective of creativity.

Chapter 5 explains meaningful ways in which to achieve full concentration. As noted earlier, the mind moves faster than light. So, remaining concentrated on one objective is the real achievement. When you achieve full concentration the mind runs at zero speed for some time. It will give you the feeling of being completely out of this world. Even a noisy environment will not disturb your concentration for long.

W5 is closely connected with concentration. Its use is explained in the question and answer format.

What is concentration?
Concentration is the process of bringing the mind to zero speed, i.e., focusing on one objective only. This is in itself an achievement.

Who should practice concentration?
Everyone should practice concentration by focusing on their desired objective. This is a must for everybody in their daily lives.

For whom should concentration be practiced?
Concentration is a subject that is of interest to society as a whole, that is to say the entire community. This is much more important than anything else.

When should concentration begin?
Concentration should be taught from the initial phases of life.

Where concentration should be practiced?
The answer is: anywhere and everywhere. But it is not really a question of practicing – it will happen automatically in time.

2.8 C5 Practice
C5 is divided into three phases as listed in Table.

Phase 1 - The first phase involves concentrating on good events that happened in the past. In the beginning you

The three phases of C5

C5 phase	Concentration without any break	Time for achieving the concentration without any break	Type of practice	Difficulty
Phase 1	5 minutes	up to 2 years	Memorize past happy events in your life. Focus on one point	Very difficult to focus
Phase 2	10 to 15 minutes	Up to 1 years	Visualize past happy events or future plans	Practice makes it easier
Phase 3	More than 30 minutes	Up to 9 months	Focus and think of innovative ideas	Full concentration for a longer period becomes easy

should concentrate on a single point, for example a spot on the wall, or the flame of a candle. After a lot of practice in concentrating for a long time, you should focus on positive events that occur in your daily life. Try to observe minute things and details. This will help you to release your tension.

This concentration period should last for five minutes. In the beginning it is especially difficult to stop other thoughts from popping up in the mind. After practicing for some weeks it becomes easier. You have to be patient and you will master this exercise in bringing calmness and peace of mind.

Phase 2 - After some practice you can increase the time span up to 10 to 15 minutes. You have to picture a thing or a symbol in front of your inner eye and shut out all thoughts that come into your mind. You should start visualizing future plans or happy events in your life.

Phase 3 - In this phase, you have to concentrate for a longer period, more than 30 minutes. Concentrate on innovative ideas. You should try to concentrate fully on a subject that you find important. Think about the subject in its full depth, then work out a solution, evaluate it in detail and try to implement your thoughts in actions in the days to come. The selected subject should be helpful in your daily

Exercise

Step 1
Open your palms as shown below and feel how you are opening yourself to God, say the following sentence:

"*O, God give me full strength to run successfully all the operations for which I am responsible by your blessing.*"

Step 2
Then join your palms together and say:

"*Generator of the universe.*"

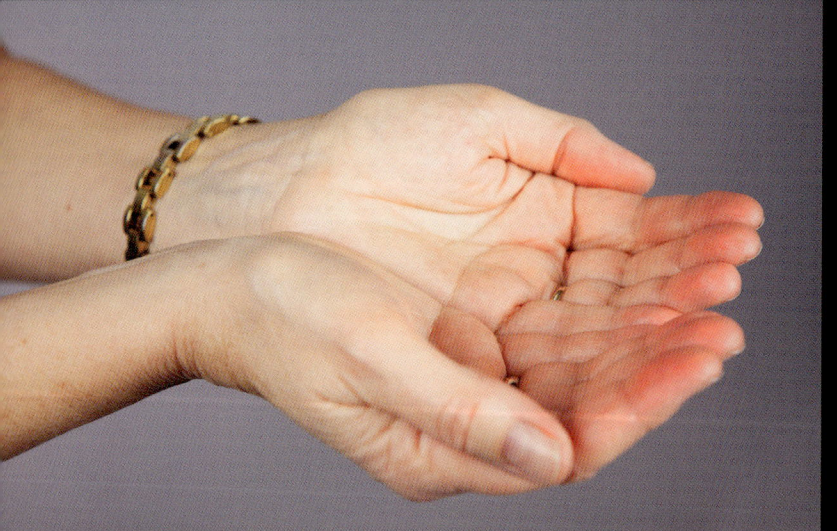

activities and the consequences of your actions should be positive.

Concentration brings you into a meditative phase and you thus gain the strength to focus on achieving your goal of personalization.

2.8.1 Practicing C5

C5 will help your body as well as your mind to achieve personalization and a good quality of life. Some extremely simple exercises that integrate physical and mental training will help you gain better control and achieve peace of mind. You need to do the exercises daily. After regular practice you will improve your control of the techniques.

Exercise

Invocation

After waking up in the morning, before you begin your daily routines, start praying to GOD. It depends on you to whom you address your prayers. When you hand over all your worries to a mighty power, you will feel stress free. Prayer is asking for support and help to achieve your goals and carry out the duties laid on you. This exercise shows your willingness to be accountable for your being.

Step 3 Fold your hands and say:

"**O**perator of the universe."

Step 4 Clench your fists and say:

"**D**estructor of all evils."

Practicing outside in nature is helpful. You can practice at home in front of an open door or an open window. Do it with full conviction.

You can practice this by repeating the sentences five times or by repeating them all together (from step 1 to step 4) five times. By uttering the sentences, combined with the actions of bringing your hands and palms together, you show respect to the Almighty, and demonstrate an understanding of the fusion of everything that is good in your world. Finally you state that bad things should be eliminated.

Breathing exercise

Deep abdominal breathing

Type 1

This is slow, deep breathing. You should inhale air slowly while counting to five, wait for five counts and then exhale. Counting should be done in the mind, not aloud. Start practicing for ten minutes at a time. You can practice many times a day anywhere and at any time, sitting in the office or while travelling. It gives a feeling of calmness and balance.

Type 2

The first exercise consists of inhaling deeply. This is 'belly breathing'. Then hold your breath for some time and breathe out slowly and say for as long as possible "OOOOOOOOOOOMMM".

This exercise should be repeated 11 times.

The second exercise is similar to the first one; this time, close your lips while you make the sound OOOOOOOOOOOOOMMM. Also this exercise should be repeated 11 times.

2.8.2 Daily routine

Start and end your day on a good note. You should always start the day in a good mood, fulfill the day's duties in that mood, and close the evening with a smile.

Plan a detailed program for the day

When the day starts you should make a program for your whole day's activities. Implement the topics designated for that day as best you can. At the end of the day, look back with satisfaction on the things that you have accomplished. Do not place the topics which you did not complete in a negative corner, but put them on the list for tomorrow and try to do the remaining topics the next day. You should strive to limit the number of points on your list so that it is realistic and you can manage to deal with all the tasks on the day's list. Take pauses to rest and exercise while you are at work.

You should make pauses in your work for doing some exercises, and you should try to introduce periods of rest in your work, body and mind. The daily program with the described morning and evening sessions will help you establish a positive structure in your daily life; your body and mind will be in balance and you will have a more positive attitude toward your personal as well as professional life. Before you start your work at the office, devote some time to carrying out a few breathing exercises as these will increase the potential and effectiveness of your work. By reserving time for moments of rest in your planning, you will allow your body and mind to relax and this helps release tension.

Repetitive counting in physical exercise
Physical exercise and walking will also help you relax. While you perform physical exercises you have no time to think about your everyday problems and this automatically diverts your attention from stressful thoughts. Counting the repetitive movements in your exercise program helps you forget the issues which are very stressful for your mind. Also going for a long walk in nature will help to release the stress of both body and mind.

Exercise for cleaning the mind
You should do some exercises during the day in order to allow your mind and body to rest during working hours. You need to have a good balance between work and rest. To clear your mind you could listen to restful, soothing music, read something relaxing, nurture a hobby or play a musical instrument. Walking in free nature also gives rest.

Concentrate and think about positive events
You should always be positive and think about positive events from your own life, such as holidays, children, etc. You have to select just one single topic and give it your full attention so that you can imagine many details related to the topic.

A happy end to the day
Before going to sleep you should go through all the things you have experienced during the day; try to think what effect these events have had on your mind; recall the positive and negative feelings that all these things passed on to your mind and why.

After regular practice of C5 you will be more observant, a better listener and feel happier and calmer – this will make you sleep better with the result that stress and tension is avoided. When you see that C5 brings these benefits, you will be inclined to continue practicing regularly.

Chapter 3

A Reality

After a long period of time, I decided to introduce the practice of C5 to a wider circle. I did not want it to remain in my mind only and thereby get lost forever. I took the first step in this process by initiating a world renowned professor in telecommunications from the Netherlands.

Chapter 3 presents the true story about the professor, whose name is Leo. His wife is called Inez.

Section 3.1 introduces Leo's background and also the basis of our common understanding.

The C5 learning process and its background story are narrated in Section 3.2. Our first meeting about C5 took place in 2002, but it was not until over a year later that we started our lessons together. That was in 2004.

Both of these meetings took place in Denmark as described in Section 3.3. Section 3.3 is very significant because it gives details about C5 practice and Leo's valuable experience, reflections and feelings about it. This is the longest section of the book.

The second C5 session was held in the Netherlands and it is described in Section 3.4.

Section 3.5 gives an account of the results and impact of C5 practice in Leo's life.

Finally conclusion and recommendations are presented in Section 3.6.

Left: Leo and I in a natural environment

3.1 Introduction

Leo[1] is the scientific director of a university institute with a staff of more than 100, consisting of full, associate and assistant professors, PhDs and Post-docs, and technical, managerial and administrative staff.

Leo has an extremely burdensome workload with work days of 12 to 16 hours. He always works seven days a week. He has no time to relax e.g. by watching the television. Only his summerhouse at the lake provides some relief because there he has the opportunity to sail.

Moments of relaxation

---

1 Comments: Leo had various contacts with doctors; their response was: "you have burned out". Leo commented "I have a nice job which I really like and it is not too hard. It just takes a lot of time'". Nobody in Leo's environment could see that there was a dysfunctional problem.

The photo shows Leo and Inez's sailing boat. The family house has become a workhouse instead of a home where there is ample time to relax.

His academic research programs are becoming bigger and bigger and he is becoming more and more involved in university and faculty politics, which is against his nature. Leo grows more and more aware of the tricks and manipulative games being played in the academic world, and he finds them disgusting. A growing institute also means more management duties but his ambitions lie in giving lectures and working with MSc and PhD students and with the technical and scientific staff.

At the same time Leo starts to work on his visionary concept of ZeZo which is to create favorable conditions for self-care for elderly people whereby they are able to stay in their own homes as long as possible with a minimum of external care. He designs an apartment house optimized for three elderly families above 55 years of age realized in 2005.

In short, Leo has an interesting life. However, there is also a dark side to this way of life: Leo cannot sleep well; he has problems concentrating and always feels tired. He told me about these problems in 2002.

I suggested that Leo should learn the C5 techniques and this awakened his interest.

3.1.1 Understanding

At our meeting in 2002 I told Leo: "I am not going to teach you now. Let's make an appointment and start during a weekend when we both have free time. We'll organize a weekend where Inez, Jyoti, you, and I have plenty of time at our disposal. During that weekend we shall do some specific exercises, but we shall also have substantial free time for relaxing, sightseeing, dinners, etc. together." Leo was flabbergasted. He had no idea why I wanted to carry out an introduction to concentration and meditation techniques at a weekend. On the one hand, Leo found it hard to believe that it was possible to solve a big problem by introducing him to an area completely unknown to him and by combining it with socializing. On the other hand, Leo was fully convinced that he should give it a go. He still remembers clearly that when he told the outcome our talk to Inez, she reacted to Leo's enthusiasm rather harshly. She did not believe that my knowledge and insight would provide answers for Leo's problem. However, she supported Leo because she also wished that his constant tiredness and his sleeping problems could be resolved. The idea that the C5 sessions could be combined with a cozy weekend was also attractive. Inez was curious about me and appreciated the good relationship Leo and I shared.

The next day Leo said, "Let's organize the first meeting". I replied, "I shall ask Jyoti to organize the first meeting. This is not so easy, because we both are pretty busy and only a few weekends are available".

I advised him not to worry about the preparations: "Just make sure that you have ample free time and don't bring along any work." Leo was ecstatic.

It had been a long time since I had taught C5 to others and I had never done any C5 sessions after leaving India. I had to prepare the sessions. In the meantime Jyoti told Leo, "Ramjee is extremely good at everything connected with concentration and meditation, much better than me". She also remarked that if Ramjee promises to help someone, she is fully confident that it will work out.

3.2 Learning process

From the time Leo accepted my offer of teaching him the relaxation techniques, 1½ years passed before we got around to organizing the first structured session. We had built up a good friendship, not just as colleagues who both work in the field of telecommunications, but also privately. Our wives, too, had established a very good relationship and therefore it would be true to say that the ties between our two families are strong and durable.

At the time Leo told me that he had a fabulous family, a very interesting job where he could do things which he really enjoyed, such as giving lectures and cooperating with students and staff; and he had established a successful institute in which large national and international programs were carried out. However, he still had one major problem: he could hardly sleep and he could not get enough rest at night.

I assured Leo that I understood his problem. However, I had never had sleeping problems myself and I had never suffered from exhaustion. I always start work very early in the morning, often at 4 o'clock. During the day I have always been a devil for work. In the evening I have time for my family and I spend any remaining time reading and writing documents, books and reports.

I told Leo that I really believed that being a professor was the best job in the world for him, as it is for me. My own ambition is to be a pioneer in advanced education and research and my position as a professor enables me to do this. Internationalization has played a prominent role in my whole career and I certainly wanted to continue the cooperation between Leo's and my own university institutes.

Leo talked about the things he did at home, things which he considered to be the most important things in life. I agreed with him and talked openly about my own family situation, my wife, children and grandchildren. Leo was puzzled by the fact that I could do so many different things each day without becoming tired. "I make a positive start when I wake up", I told him. "During the day I take short intensive pauses to rest (about 10 to 20 minutes) and those moments help me get through the day's meetings, problems, etc. without getting exhausted. I close my day before bedtime and with just a few hours of deep sleep, I have always fully recovered from a hard day's work by the next morning." Leo didn't believe that it would work for him in the same way. He was skeptical and thought that such a way of life would have too big an impact on his normal way of life. I replied, "I can help you, but you really must be open for this kind of life yourself". Leo said that he was interested, but that nevertheless he worried that after the sessions with me, his normal, everyday life with sleepless nights and a constant feeling of exhaustion would just continue.

After this first discussion Leo's workload got heavier and heavier. He took on the task of designing and building a big house with three apartments while continuing to initiate national and international activities at the university, planning many trips, etc. Leo often thought about what I had told him. He tried to have rest breaks during the day, but failed. The results did not satisfy him, and each day after work Leo was dog-tired and he continued to have problems sleeping. Only during the winter sports holidays was he able to get some rest. During the holidays he thought about his demanding position but this did not result in his finding a way of solving his problems of feeling tired constantly and of not getting enough sleep. He realized that he was becoming more and more interested in my concept. When we met Leo would immediately start discussing his attempts to create moments of rest during the day. He had found the idea interesting but he had often found it difficult to put it into practice. Leo's life was in a rut. He asked me how I could avoid getting exhausted after a long day's work. I told him that it was because of C5. I told him about my youth in India. During the intelligent phase of life, I had practiced C5 by doing concentration and meditation exercises; and later, but still at a young age, I had practiced as a teacher. Even at that young age I taught my approach to people mostly older than me using my own experience. After a long discussion I decided that I would be willing to teach Leo everything about the C5 concept which I had refined and developed in the course of the previous decades for my own benefit. I wanted to teach Leo and maybe a second friend, but not others because I was a very busy person myself and I also had an extremely heavy work load.

Leo indicated that he had read a little about meditation as practiced in the Far East. He found it rather woolly and vague and difficult to implement in his daily life. He did not believe that it could have much impact on him. Leo is a straight-forward thinking person and fuzzy ideas do not fit in his outlook on life. I listened carefully and patiently to his skepticism. I reassured him he too could reach the point where C5 became part of his life. I advised him to stop reading literature about meditation. "You must experience it and I shall let you experience the specific C5 approach." Leo was astonished by this answer. He was relieved because he knew it was much easier to learn something by experiencing it in practice than getting knowledge by reading. Trying to learn about meditation through books had raised more questions than answers. He said that if he really could take part in practical exercises to learn about C5 he would be very grateful. I had to tell him, "I am not 100% certain how it will affect you, but it is certain that something will happen". Leo was disconcerted and impressed at the same time and did not know what to think.

3.3 First series of sessions in 2004[2]

Jyoti and I made all the necessary preparations for Leo's introductory C5 weekend session. Jyoti had reserved hotel rooms in North Jutland in Denmark. It was said to be a very suitable place for what we wanted to do during this first C5 weekend. The week before his departure Leo had all kinds of thoughts about what could happen that weekend. These ranged from difficult physical and/or yoga exercises to mental training in concentration and meditation. Inez and Leo decided to travel by car so that they had ample time to discuss what could be expected in that weekend. They left home on the Thursday afternoon and spent the night in a hotel near the German-Danish border. During the trip Leo told Inez that he was uncertain and nervous: uncertain because he was still skeptical about whether C5 would help him overcome his tiredness and his sleeping problems, and nervous because he sometimes felt that he was escaping into the unknown just because he hoped that his problems could be reduced. Leo could not rely on himself but had to trust me and he found it hard to do this without any proof that the experiment would have a positive effect. As a scientist, Leo considered the experiment as vague and poorly defined, without well-described goals, a time schedule and milestones with measurable intermediate or ultimate results.

---

[2] Comment: In the months up to that first weekend, Leo was convinced that something had to be done to solve his problems. However, the closer the date of the weekend drew near the more doubts came into his mind. His thoughts the week before the weekend were so mixed that Leo became confused. For this reason a summary is given on Leo's struggle to order his thoughts before the weekend. It is noteworthy that Leo's thoughts changed after just one day of experiencing C5.
Looking back four years after that first weekend, Leo said that what he had expected before he had had the first C5 experience was completely different from what happened. Actually, after the first series of sessions with me that weekend, but certainly even more so after several years of weekend sessions, Leo had to admit that he had had to adjust his point of view; in particular he had learned that I wanted to help him, not just by standard yoga but by offering the C5 concept, and that C5 is a combination of philosophy, belief and science, with a set of concrete activities and actions leading to an increased impact over time.

That Thursday, Inez and Leo's discussions focused mainly on the uncertain aspects. Inez, too, had her reservations; she is a very no-nonsense type of person who always gives her honest opinion. In the evening they promised each other to start the weekend with a positive attitude. Leo should inform Inez in detail about his feelings during and after the weekend sessions with me; Inez was to help him evaluate any developments.

Furthermore, they both felt that they should not have too high expectations; some of the terms that cropped up in their discussions were: "You never know" and "We'll give it a chance".

Next morning after breakfast they started the last part of their trip. It was splendid weather, almost as if this was meant to contribute to suppressing their skepticism. They were glad that they both supported this experiment, and they looked forward to spending a nice weekend with friends.

Inez and Leo arrived at the hotel around noon. The hotel was situated in the countryside. It looked like an isolated castle at the end of a long driveway. Leo's first impression was: "What a beautiful setting in the middle of nowhere". Inez and Leo were impressed by the part Jyoti in particular had played in making this first weekend a very special one by selecting a hotel in an overwhelmingly tranquil environment.

As Inez and Leo were unloading their luggage from the car Jyoti and I came out of the main entrance of the hotel to give them a hearty welcome. It was a very good start: a very warm welcome among friends at the beginning of a weekend full of unknowns for Leo.

After Inez and Leo had checked in they went to their room which was next to ours. It was at the end of a corridor in the wing of the castle and so it was isolated and quiet. The rooms were furnished with antiques and located in a part of the castle which was kept in the original style with low doors and small windows. The room and the furniture gave one the feeling of stepping out of 21st century and into the 18th century.

I had organized a welcome drink on the terrace.

Happy moment in a long series

After that we had lunch and it must be said that the atmosphere was excellent. In the afternoon we went on an excursion to the beach. During our walk Leo wanted to discuss my plans for the weekend. I did not give many details; I only said: "We start early tomorrow morning" and, "This first day is important for creating an optimal atmosphere". Then we returned to the castle where we had a luxury aperitif followed by a splendid dinner. We did not discuss the activities that were to take place the next morning.

That evening Leo thought about what he should expect the next morning: it could be a 'soft' approach, some understanding, me listening to Leo's stories, some meditation, physical exercises, etc. Leo really had no idea what would happen.

Next morning Leo and I woke early. He was still puzzled, a bit anxious and slightly suspicious. I knocked on his door at the appointed time and he noticed that I had some kind of hold on him. It looked as though I wanted to say 'I have everything under control'. I did not speak much, only a few short sentences. We both walked slowly away from the castle; I was searching for a restful place. As we walked something unforgettable started for Leo.

For Leo, walking along that trail awakened a kind of consciousness of the beauty of nature and the blessing of rest and silence. We could hear birds, the rustle of leaves on the trees and could see colorful flowers on the path and in the meadow. From far away came the faint sounds of agricultural machinery.

I walked slowly, on and on, until we lost sight of the hotel. Leo walked beside me and did not know how far we would be going. We did not say much to each other. In the beginning Leo made some remarks about the weather, about nature, etc., rather non-important issues. He too became more and more quiet. Then Leo remembered that I was making ready for the exercises. He became conscious of the fact that in a world where the pace is very fast, moments of rest are of great value. For Leo this first experience was an adventure, but nevertheless he had no real insight into the process that had actually begun.[3]

After a while, Leo started wondering whether we were only going to make a silent tour during that first session or whether I had something else on the program. At one point I stopped. We had arrived at an idyllic spot. I said: "Here we will make a stop. This is an excellent location for our body and mind". Leo also felt that the location was ideal for the purpose. There was silence again. Half a minute, one minute, it was a non-measurable time span in which a high level of tension built up. Then I asked: "Do you believe in God". Oops! Such a question was unexpected for Leo. He did not know whether he could simply answer with a yes or a no. He wondered if he should give a clarification. Many thoughts crossed his mind at great speed. At the same time

---

3 Nowadays, more than four years later, it must be said that creating silence and rest in hectic everyday life is of immense value. It you are able to reconfigure your own environment by stimulating all related sensors in your mind and body (which normally are not activated) you can evoke the wanted images. By recalling and experiencing once again beautiful previous events by activating those special sensors you can reach extraordinary results. This can be stated so strongly because Leo experienced the huge significance of creating such an environment. The result was that by doing so, after three or four years Leo was able to have good moments during the day and could fully relax. Place and time are then of no importance.

Leo became more and more aware of the paradisiacal environment in which we found ourselves where not a trace of the hustle and bustle of life could be heard. Leo simply said: "yes"[4].

His 'yes' was enough for me. I replied: "I also believe in God". All was quiet again. Leo had the feeling that there was a strong link between us and he knew that the link was a very good one. (Four years later, Leo told me that all the details of this first event were warm and good, but that this was something that he had realized much later).

Then I said: "Open the palms of your hands and repeat what I say and do this five times". Leo opened his palms and felt openness toward God. I said in a soft voice: "O, God give me full strength to run successfully all the operations that I achieved by your blessing."[5] Leo repeated the sentence, also in a soft voice. We said this sentence for a second, third, fourth and fifth time. It was a revelation.

Leo got a sense of well-being while asking God for support in everything he was doing and for everything he was accountable for.

Again there was silence. Leo realized that we were at one with our paradisiacal environment. It was a special experience. Since that day Leo has said this sentence five times a day, mostly in the morning, when he is still in bed. As he repeats the sentence he recalls the happy moments when we walked together during the first session in that overwhelmingly tranquil and idyllic natural environment.

I then said; "Do the next exercise also five times". I added, "Join the palms of your hands together and say": "*Generator of the universe*". Fold the palms of your hands together and say: "*Operator of the universe*". Then clench the palms of your hands and say: "*Destructor of all evils*".

Leo repeated the actions and said these sentences with full conviction. The initial letters of the three sentences make the word "GOD" and that impressed him.

You show respect to the Almighty by both uttering the above sentences and by joining your palms together. Then you represent the fusion of everything good in your world. Finally, you say that bad things should be eliminated. This

---

4 He said 'yes' because his world view had been built up with God during all his life. It was stimulated by his parents in his youth and further strengthened in the many years following where the sense of life, love and care had found a place in his existence. Thanks to the change in Leo's life brought about by C5, his belief in God has also deepened and achieved another dimension. At every start or end of the day, God is in his mind. Also during moments of rest during the day God penetrates his mind. It does not mean that many prayers are said to contact God. No, it happens during the moments of concentration and meditation where his thoughts are directed toward the most beautiful gifts and achievements of life, i.e. his wife, marriage, children, grandchildren, their love, their gratitude, their warmth, their feelings, the atmosphere when the family is gathered, but also toward his health, job, national and international colleagues, and personnel with whom he has daily contact. Every time he thinks about those beautiful gifts some thoughts come into his mind where God is giving directions.

5 Comment: background info see Chapter 1

A C5 Session

exercise gave Leo a guideline for obedience and willingness to be accountable for his being.

The picture shows our first C5 session. It is probably no longer necessary to point out that Leo had not anticipated such an event. It had a special effect on the way he functioned from that moment. He felt different from before. For the duration of those 15 to 20 minutes all his worries were banished from his mind; what had seemed very important the day before, was no longer so.

Leo seemed to have discovered a new yardstick with which to measure the importance of his thoughts. He tried to explain his thoughts to me. I said, "The real mind exercises are still to come. We must do two extra exercises of a total of ten minutes. The first one clears the mind for five minutes. After this you should concentrate fully on an important topic for five minutes. You must think about the topic in its full depth, then work it out, evaluate it in detail and try to transform your thoughts into actions to be performed in the days to come. The selected subject should contribute positively to your daily life activities and lead to positive and pleasant actions".

Leo found these two exercises pretty tough. Why? He had never done this sort of exercise before. He was not aware of what to expect and had no references. He had no idea how and where to start clearing his mind. Leo closed his eyes; he was to think of nothing. But Leo was unable to do that. He had too many thoughts going through his mind. He thought about this exciting moment, the environment and himself. However, after a few minutes all kind of ideas and thoughts started racing through his mind. He had the feeling that this could not be the real purpose. In private and in work situations Leo is always a thinker who tries to get fast results from his deliberations. Now he was to suppress his manifold thoughts and he was to produce the "result" in a very short time. It was against his nature and created difficulties which he could not overcome at that moment.[6]

In conclusion, Leo found it rather difficult to stay concentrated during this first session of mind clear-

---

6 After this weekend event Leo went home and four months passed before he experienced the first tricks of cleaning the mind and concentrating fully on one subject. Day by day he improved his control over these techniques. It must be mentioned here that the learning process of cleaning the mind and full concentration gave Leo a most important challenge. He finally got the knack of this process by using C5 extensively. This happened after two years of intensive exercising and by integrating physical and mental training.

ing and concentration exercises. Leo was so used (and often still is) to being a devil for work in short periods. To stand still for five minutes to concentrate fully on one subject seemed trivial, but it is not[7]. After cleaning the mind and completing the full concentration exercises, Leo discussed his experiences briefly. I told him to let it rest for a while. We continued with a last series of exercises. These were breathing exercises.

The first exercise consists of inhaling deeply, the so-called 'belly breathing'. You hold your breath for some time and then breathe out slowly saying OOOOOOOOOOMMM as long as possible.

This exercise should be repeated 11 times.

The second exercise is similar to the first one, but the lips stay closed while you make the noise OOOOOOOOOOOOMMM. Also this exercise should be repeated 11 times.

Both exercises brought back the atmosphere which was created during the first phase, before we started the cleaning and full concentration session. After this last exercise Leo looked at me. He had had a special feeling and he thanked me for such a unique first perception. We walked back to the hotel and did not say much. Afterward, Leo could not remember precisely what happened during our walk back. He was full of all impressions from the first session, which had lasted only 40 minutes.

When we returned to the hotel Leo felt very relaxed. He went to his hotel room where Inez asked how things had gone. Leo just said that what had happened was very special, but that he could not perform all the exercises perfectly.

Both families went for breakfast and we had an excellent day. The atmosphere was perfect and we all enjoyed our stay thoroughly.

We used the early mornings of the next two days in the same way as the first morning. Leo and I did our exercises. I emphasized that Leo should have patience in order to have sufficient success in cleaning the mind and doing the full concentration exercises[8].

What was special about the first weekend was that the early morning sessions were intense but short. Within one hour we were back from the session and the rest of the day was devoted to enjoying each other's company. We discussed our plans for the day at the extensive breakfast – whether it would be a walk, a car trip, sightseeing, etc. We walked in the marshland, along the beach, visited museums, had good lunches, and enjoyed evenings with good conversation and perfect dinners. That first weekend, Leo noticed that he was full of mental barriers. He found it hard to talk about the morning sessions, or confess that he was busy

---

7 Leo had many discussions with me about these difficulties later on.

8 It turned out I was right. It took months and progress was so slow that Leo did not experience any change from one day to the next. He had to continue repeating the exercises day after day. After a few months, when he had had his first experience of being able to clean his mind and of being fully concentrated, he was very grateful that all his efforts had not been in vain. After more than two years, Leo could do these exercises to his own satisfaction.

dealing with the sessions the whole day. Regularly all kinds of thoughts came into his mind and he wondered (to his surprise) why the different exercises were so meaningful while the cleaning of the mind and full concentration exercises in particular were so difficult. He wanted to be able to have control over all the exercises as fast as possible.

I explained how important the exercises were for him personally. Leo, who also wanted to reach an ultimate understanding, was frustrated because he could not manage. He had to train himself again and again. Leo realized during that first weekend that it would cost him much effort. He was not sure if he had the strength to do it, although he had the discipline. I had already made clear in the first session that the early morning sessions could also be done immediately after he woke up. This would make it more convenient for him. I proposed that we did some exercises during the day in order to give the mind and body some rest during working hours. Leo and I also spent time on reaching moments of full concentration.

How he was to organize all this when he would be on his own was a big question for Leo, but he promised himself to put a lot of effort in getting it done. I explained that I start very early in the morning with similar exercises to the ones I had taught him, but that I also performed some special relaxation exercises during the day. I am so skilled in this that I can practice C5 in very short breaks of less than ten minutes. This is how I get through a vast amount of work without getting exhausted by the end of the day.

Leo was intrigued by how I had discovered all those effects myself. The young age at which I had started practicing C5 enabled me to control C5 perfectly. After some years I had experienced that I had reached a top level and that others recognized this. This was why people in my surroundings asked me to train them in C5, even though I was still rather young. Later, I evaluated my way of life and my practice of C5 principles. Because I wished to reach the top of my scientific field internationally I did not continue my activities as a C5 master. I maintained my C5 skills by doing exercises regularly. For many years I was of the conviction that I could demonstrate the impact of C5 and the role it can play in the daily lives of modern human beings.

Leo and I discussing C5 concept

I did not practice my C5 mastership until I offered to help Leo get over his fatigue and sleeping problems by training him in C5. I was fully convinced that I was able to become Leo's C5 master. Leo had gratefully accepted any help that could solve his problems. (At the time he had not suspected that his problems would lay the foundations of a project where the applied C5 techniques would be described in a book. From the very beginning I had thought that Leo should describe his experiences with C5 as part of a book.) After some years Leo was convinced that I knew where we started, and also knew where we wanted to come to at the end[9].

On the last evening of our first weekend we made an evaluation. Leo felt uncertain. In his professional life, this was unusual for him. He was uncertain because he still had a number of unanswered questions.

1. Can I do the exercises every day, not just in the early morning but also during the day?
2. Do I have the discipline to reach those moments of ecstasy and rest without my C5 master?
3. Can I improve my results in clearing the mind and in the full concentration exercises?

I gave Leo a very practical solution: we should organize regular telephone sessions. During those sessions we would be able to exchange ideas and thoughts but also discuss problems about lack of progress. Leo definitely wanted to make use of this offer, not so much during his daily sessions, but particularly for reporting what was going well during the exercises and what was not.

I commented: "Either you call or I call. It does not matter. We have made a start and regular contact in the first coming months is essential". I fully trusted that the experiment would be successful, especially because Leo is so disciplined in his daily life. The next morning the two families said farewell. The ladies had enjoyed the weekend very much and Leo and I promised that the first step in our tele-approach to our future C5 cooperation should be taken very soon. Leo's mind was full of the experiences he had encountered during the long weekend. It is said that time flies sometimes without us being able to remember exactly what has happened every day. However this weekend was so intense that even after several years many small details are indelibly printed in Leo's memory.

It was a very successful first experiment and Leo and I were satisfied with the results. Besides the sessions, our two families had had a relaxing and enjoyable weekend with not too much talk about our work at the universities. This also was a special experience for Leo. Leo admitted that it was very worthwhile. He had firmly resolved that only the fundamentals of C5 had been explained. At the same time he had the feeling that once in a while I was still connected with my work at the university because I had to organize several business calls or to answer incoming calls.

Another positive outcome of the weekend was the good relationship that grew between the two families. It was a little miracle that such friendship, warmth and good atmosphere came together in just one weekend. Leo felt the same way

---

9 I indicated to Leo already in the first session that several annual sessions were needed in order for him to enjoy the maximum impact of C5.

about it. During the return trip Leo and Inez did a lot of talking. Inez had been rather skeptical about the role C5 could play in solving Leo's problem. She had also tried to dampen Leo's enthusiasm a bit because she was afraid that Leo might expect too much from C5 and that he would then become disappointed if the desired result was not reached. However, she was not negative as she hoped that C5 could give Leo's body and mind a good rest. She therefore supported Leo's efforts to learn the C5 techniques. Leo knew that their mutual love would make it possible to obtain optimum success from this project. It turned out that two visions were brought together; Leo's extreme enthusiasm and Inez' ability to put things into perspective.

The morning after he reached home Leo started with a kind of relaxation exercise before doing the exercises described in the first session – with discouraging results. On the following days he made a great effort to do his exercises in the early morning, walking outside and doing exercises in bed. It was certainly not comparable with the sessions we had done during the weekend. After a week Leo called me and told me that clearing the mind and getting fully concentrated was far from easy. I explained that he should be less impatient. In a long phone call I spent most of the time giving explanations and this was different from our joint sessions in the first weekend. I gave hints on how to clear the mind by listening to restful music or reading something relaxing or doing your hobby. After that I proposed that he took a walk in the countryside.

After some preparation Leo should start with the concentration exercises and think about positive events from his daily life, such as holidays, children, etc. "Select just one topic and give it all your attention" and "Try to recall a lot of details connected with the topic" was my advice. After this telephone consultation he spent a considerable amount of time on the exercises. He persevered in his attempts but had the impression that he was not making very much progress. After a week I called and asked him about his progress. Leo felt that there was not much change. "Carry on with your exercises" and "You are doing well", I simply said to him.

Leo in a concentrated mood

Leo answered: "I certainly shall do that". I started to explain what to do according to the same pattern. In the next few days Leo proceeded with the exercises we had discussed, in the early morning and during working hours. A week later I called him again. Leo could not see whether there had been any progress. I said, "The way you are talking about this now indicates that there has been some progress". Why did Leo not experience this? He did not want to seem desperate, but sometimes he had the feeling that he was stuck. After several months and many phone calls, sometimes with intervals of more than one week between them because one of us was abroad, I made it clear to him that there was certainly noticeable progress. I made a comparison between the results Leo reported at this stage with what he had gained from the first weekend session. I then demonstrated that I was able to maintain the images from the first session and how Leo had developed. This ability was extremely valuable because without stimulation from me there was a risk that Leo could not go on doing his exercises. It was Leo's own experience that after four months the clearing exercises went automatically, while the full concentration exercises were still too difficult. After five to six months Leo thought that the full concentration exercises were also going a bit smoother and they gave him more satisfaction. He carried out all the exercises strictly, in exactly the same way as we had done the exercises the first weekend. Doing the exercises according to a structure helped Leo. He felt good about doing this series of tasks every day. However, his sleeping problems had still not been resolved. There were some nights where he slept a bit better, but he had still not had a full night's sleep.

Leo understood that he should be satisfied with the fact that he felt better and this was in itself an achievement. His working hours were extremely long at the time. He worked around 100 hours per week and had hardly any time for relaxation in the way he had done that weekend with me. I suggested that in 2005, at our next weekend session with the two families, I should offer some new exercises to help him get a better balance between work and rest. Leo continued his efforts with the existing exercises but he was also very eager to know about the new ones.

3.4 Second series of sessions in 2005

A year after the first weekend session Inez and Leo organized a weekend in a castle resort in the Netherlands. The circumstances were also ideal, i.e. we could walk in the castle garden and there were isolated places for doing C5 exercises. In the first early morning session I asked Leo to do as he did every morning. The exercises were those that I had shown him, and which made Leo feel the atmosphere of our first weekend. It was not the same as doing the exercises at home. It looked as though we were in the same situation as the year before. There was a difference, however. It was Leo who showed me how he did his exercises and I followed. The atmosphere was very special. Leo told me this. After that he told me about his working situation which took up all his energies. I said: "Tomorrow I shall explain what kind of new exercises you can do". Leo could hardly wait for that moment. After the early morning session both families had a relaxing day together. We went to islands off the coast, bicycled, and had a nice lunch and dinner. Leo was fishing for my plans: he had no idea what they were, but I had.

Next morning we walked again along a beautiful trail and coming to the selected spot I said, "You should always start

the day in a good mood, you should fulfill the duties of the day in a good mood and you should close the evening in a good mood". Leo thought for a while and then asked, "Please explain". I replied, "It is rather simple. When the day starts you make a program for what you want to do that day or what you should do that day, then execute the tasks indicated on the list for that day as well as you can. At the end of the day, look back with satisfaction to the subjects you carried out successfully that day. Place those topics which you did not complete in a negative corner, but put them on the list for tomorrow and try to do the remaining topics the next day. Next, you should put fewer points on your list so that you have a realistic chance of completing all of them. Make room for pauses in your work, do some exercises and try to bring rest into your work, body and mind".

It was an eye-opener for Leo to start the day in a positive way, but also to close the day in the same manner. This allows you to do much more than just completing the activities that come along that day. Because combining the ad-hoc activities with the activities already recorded on your agenda can create stress. Ending the day on a positive note is of great significance. That morning we came back a little later than usual because we did our 'standard exercises' as well as discussing the manifold topics Leo had raised.

Leo was very interested in how to go about making a program list for the day, keeping in mind that

The second meeting

he works in an environment where it is important that he is available for people who need to see him. Leo explained the reality of his working day. The people at the university and the institute he directs are his main priority. His motto has always been: "People are the most important" and "The hardware and the software are not important, but the brainware is." Leo has no PC in his office because he does not want to sit behind a screen all day dealing with emails, reading documents, and responding to the outside world via computer communication. All his emails are received by the institute secretariat and at home. Leo reads his emails at home and Inez often writes the responses following Leo's instructions. Inez is also involved in archiving. Some emails contain a request for an interview. Discussions with the institute's personnel take place in 'real life' meetings. The same applies to discussions on documents, reports, publications, minutes of meetings, etc. When a discussion is called for Leo always uses personal communication. This approach has helped Leo create a good working atmosphere. While this gives him a great deal of satisfaction, it costs him a lot of time. He is therefore rather interested in a more efficient way of working and wants to close his day in a positive mood.

Leo had many more questions for me – he wanted to hear about my way of working, and which exercises I do myself at the beginning and during the day. I get up every day between 4 and 5 o'clock in the morning and start doing my C5 exercises. The session lasts about 45 minutes. Then I read reports, publications, books, etc., or talk to international colleagues and leaders of institutes and companies worldwide by phone. Leo's impression is that I have worked already a full day before others start their day. After my morning activities, and when I am not on a trip, Jyoti takes me to the institute. I do not have a driver's license. Jyoti is like Inez acting as my support in everything I undertake. As soon as I arrive at the institute I take a moment's rest and meditate. Leo said that he wanted to learn to do this but so far he was not able to reach the right stage in meditation for five to ten minutes. For that reason Leo needed to take longer pauses during the day, 15 minutes or more. During those pauses Leo should evaluate all the things which he had already accomplished and the things which he still needed to do. On other occasions Leo preferred doing concentration exercises because he felt that he was more alert in his work afterward.

Leo and I returned late for breakfast. The ladies had already started. Jyoti and Inez could see that Leo and I had done a lot of talking and during breakfast the four of us discussed the topics which had come up during the early morning session. That day we made a long bike trip through the dunes. After our return to the hotel Leo and I continued to discuss concrete examples of activities which play a role in both our careers, such as the need for establishing and/or further developing big associations in the scientific world. The evening session of the second day was devoted to ways of closing the day in a positive mood. Leo did this partly in direct communication with me, and partly when he was in bed. Next morning he did some mental exercise, making a program for the day to come. The positive elements, the things that gave him greatest satisfaction, filled his mind. The early morning session that day went in the same way as the day before, but it was shorter. Again a special atmosphere was created between us and as we walked back Leo thanked me for all the things that he had already achieved. However, his sleeping problem had still not been solved.

3.5 The impact and results of Leo's activities and experiences with C5

3.5.1 The C5 concept for Leo in the beginning

I explained the term C5 to Leo in the months following our first meeting. Leo and I had regular long talks on the phone. On the days when Leo had no telephone contact with me, he had imaginary contact and discussions. The topics of the discussions during these imaginary phone calls were particularly related to Leo's difficulty in performing the mind clearing exercises. Leo imagined that I gave him various suggestions, such as "if it last less than five minutes that is fine" or "stop in case you have the feeling that it is not really working" or "relax before the exercises" or "take a walk outside" or "try to guide yourself away from the day to day worries", etc.

3.5.2 First year

In the first year, Leo spent 20 minutes every morning on the day's program - concentration exercises, meditation, breathing and prayers to the Almighty.

In general the daily program consisted of the following topics:

- New plans for the day
- Plans not executed the day before
- Plans for the day's meetings

Every evening Leo spent 30 minutes doing some concentration and meditation exercises and closed the day by summarizing the plans that had been executed and those that had to wait for next day.

The **advantages** of such a daily program for Leo were:

a. A firm program with fixed parts.
b. Reserving time for C5 every day.
c. Starting and closing the day in a private environment.
d. Sometimes long telephone sessions with me.

The **disadvantages** for Leo were:

a. A fixed structure of the day often leads to a recurrence of topics in the concentration and meditation exercises
b. Leo was not always in the mood for cleaning his mind and filling it afterward without taking his daily problems into consideration. This aspect sometimes gave Leo a sense of disappointment
c. A lack of discipline to reserve time every morning and evening for the exercises
d. Many topics in concentration and meditation exercises often repeat themselves. The topics are mostly spoken out in his mind like prayers. Leo often had the impression that many of the day's new experiences hardly played a role in the morning and evening sessions
e. Leo only did the things I advised him to do, meaning that there was very little own input.

3.5.3 Later years

After the experience of the first year we extended the morning session by ten minutes, adding the topics to be handled that day.

The daily program with morning and evening sessions helped Leo structure his daily life in a better way, and this created a more positive attitude toward his colleagues and family. However, his biggest problem remained unsolved, namely his inability to rest his mind. Dealing with the issues that cropped up in his daily life took him too long time. Leo did not want these thoughts to impact too much on his life. He noted that especially in the morning session it was difficult to clear his mind. He felt that he did not use the correct technique to handle this problem. The result was that after one year of experience he still had difficulty in getting a full night's sleep and the necessary rest.

At the same time Leo still had many duties at work as well as in his private life. Working weeks of around 100 hours were still no exception. Leo discussed this with me during our yearly meetings where Jyoti, Inez, Leo and I spent a long weekend in a castle resort with a beautiful big garden. I proposed that I should not introduce any new exercises, but that Leo should continue his daily training in more or less the same way. In the morning session in the garden Leo and I did the exercises that Leo usually did at home. After a nice day together, Leo talked to me about the day's experiences (evaluating the positive events of that day, the talks during our walk, etc.). However, he alone chose the subject he would think about in the evening session before going to sleep. I made clear that Leo's problem was understandable but a bit worrying. Leo should find more moments of rest during the day. I gave him the following advice:

a. Before starting work in the office, do some breathing exercises and also reserve some time for creating moments of rest
b. During the day do some physical exercise such as taking a walk

Leo told me that this was easier said than done.

Almost two years later Leo had a heart attack. He spent three days in intensive care and two weeks in the medium care department of the hospital. Leo had experienced a 'near death' moment that made a huge impact on his life. This extreme experience laid the foundation for giving priority to working toward giving his mind more rest. In the hope of achieving better concentration and meditation, he frantically took up his exercises again. During his heart rehabilitation program he was advised not to do any heavy physical exercise. Leo was uncomfortable and very unhappy about the situation. Before his stroke he had been in good physical condition.

A few months later we held our third annual meeting of the two families, this time organized by Jyoti and myself. This was in 2006. The first day started rather emotionally. Leo was not happy. We had a good lunch with nice wines in a restaurant overlooking a bay and later on we took a long walk. I told Leo during that walk that I could heal his mind. I listened to him and indicated that unhappy feelings cannot be solved by fanatical exercising in daily sessions. There is only one solution, to ensure that the body and mind are in equilibrium. That evening Leo became motivated anew to combine physical with mental exercise. He decided to participate in the extensive physical training offered by the heart rehabilitation program and to combine this with his morning and evening C5 sessions.

From Leo's point of view the important issue of this third annual meeting was to find a way out of an emotionally difficult situation and find a way of resting his mind. Leo is still very grateful to me for offering him a 'mental anchor' in order to find the best solution.

Despite his worsened physical condition, Leo felt that the moment had come to make a switch so that his body and mind could recover by using C5 intensively.

After 2½ years, Leo joined the hospital's heart rehabilitation program where cardiologist, physiotherapists and sport doctors were available. Leo learned via body sensing just how much physical training he could stand. This gave him a lot of self-confidence. He found that physical exercise such as biking, rowing, and team sports like handball, volleyball, under the supervision of specialists, helped him to get rid of his daily worries and gave him renewed trust in being able to stay active, physically as well as mentally. In that period Leo had two experiences which were important later on.

1. In the sports centers Leo saw many young sportsmen doing all kinds of exercises for a long period of time and realized that they had therefore no time to think about their daily problems
2. When Leo did specific physical exercises in the morning while counting the repetitive movements of each exercise, this counting helped him to forget the issues which filled his mind at that moment. This experience was not unique. Later Leo talked about this with many of his friends and nearly all of them had had similar experiences.

Based on this discovery he filled his daily morning program with a physical exercise program and maintained his morning and evening concentration and meditations sessions. He found that the combination of physical and mental programs brought his mind more rest.

After three or four years our yearly meetings focused on more variety and the improved effects of the concentration and meditation exercises. These exercises were based on my experience. The point here is that I explained the underlying vision and techniques that I myself have used for years. The idea of writing a book came to me as a result of the many in-depth discussions we had. I wanted to combine my vision, technique and experiences with Leo and Inga's experiences, Inga being the second person who also received therapy using my theory.

3.6 Conclusions and recommendations

Chapter 3 is a summary of how C5 was experienced in reality. C5 is a concept that can only be fully understood if it is based on facts. Everyone can practice it.

It has been shown that doing regular physical exercises is nearly as important as the mental exercises. Leo has now managed to achieve a state of total balance in his body and mind and he is sleeping better, he is more active nowadays throughout the day and has resumed his duties, working 60 to 80 hours per week without any problem.

Leo recommended writing an exhaustive book of over 200 pages for a clear understanding of C5 concept.

Chapter 4

"Nature provides everything; therefore you should create a natural surrounding around yourself"

A Truth

A real case story is discussed in Chapter 3. Chapter 4 presents a second case story featuring my neighbor in Denmark, Inga. I gave her the first C5 course in August 2008. She picked it up very quickly and in a short time she realized that the C5 concept is really a way of finding the truth.

When I discussed the book with her, she agreed to write a short chapter about her experience after following the initial C5 program for 8 months.

Section 4.1 introduces Inga's background. Section 4.2 describes her thoughts about her goals.

Practicing C5 is presented in Section 4.3 and finally the impact factor is explained in Section 4.4.

4.1 Inga's background

When Jyoti and I moved to Gistrup (Aalborg) in September 1999 we became Inga's neighbors. Inga and her husband came with a bouquet of flowers to welcome us. This is how Jyoti and I met Inga and her husband. They opened their arms to us in friendship. At the time Inga's husband was very ill, suffering from cancer. It was a great support for Inga to have friends like us nearby.

Inga is now a retired teacher. She stopped teaching in 2001 to be at home with her husband who died a year later in 2002. In such a situation it is very important having a strong personal network, which she luckily had, but it takes time getting used to being alone. She did not have any children. After the funeral she thought of selling the house. But then it was a great comfort to live in a place where she and her husband had shared so many good memories.

Left: Inga and I discussing C5 concept

After some time, I asked her to teach me Danish. Soon after starting, it became clear that I frequently had to cancel the lessons because of work, so Jyoti started to learn instead of me. After some time my daughter, Neeli, and daughter-in-law, Mayuri, started learning Danish, too.

Inga enjoyed teaching Danish to my family. She found that when you teach someone with a different cultural background, you learn a lot yourself and this is what happened for Inga, as she has spent many hours teaching my family.

One day when Inga was chatting with Jyoti she said that she did not feel very safe in her house after her husband's death. Especially at night, she woke up several times and thought she heard strange sounds in the house. Very often there was a natural explanation for these sounds; it could be a twig striking against the windowpane or a bird landing on the roof but enough to wake her up and keep her awake for hours. She honestly said, she had never been a sound sleeper, but after her husband's death it had become worse. When Jyoti heard about her problems she said that she was sure I could help her and that she would ask me if I would do so.

So in August 2008 I started teaching her C5, instead of her teaching me Danish. Since then we have had 15 meetings and I have taught her how, by means of some simple exercises, you can gain more control and peace of mind.

On August 16, 2008 we had our first meeting and had a long talk regarding Inga's problems. She told me that she felt stressed even though she could not find a reason for it. She did not go to work anymore and for most of the time she only had herself to consider. She had joined a class to

C5 lesson in the garden

learn Italian and often went to the cinema, concerts and opera. These things gave her joy and pleasure temporarily. So she felt the importance of C5 from a long-term perspective.

The C5 lesson is given in an outdoor environment as shown in the photograph above.

The first thing I told Inga to do was to find herself a short-term objective, something that could be achieved within half a year. As Inga could not think of anything right away I gave her eight days to think it over. Inga found out that a possible stress factor could be that she never got to the bottom of clearing out the cupboards and drawers in her house, and that she felt ashamed of this. Inga remembered that she always asked her pupils in school to clear up the classroom and their private drawers before they went home, because external mess very often was a sign of inner mess! And here she was not able to live up to her own principles. I thought that it was a very good idea and she started clearing out a little bit every day, some days only for half an hour. It was practical and gave her great satisfaction. Inga really succeeded in getting through the whole house in less than the six months and she felt very proud of herself. The effect of the C5 lessons was very positive in a short time.

4.2 Thoughts about goals

When Inga first heard that I wanted her to find a goal for herself, she did not know what to do. Inga thought it was because she had always connected the word goal with ambition and in her opinion; ambition is not something entirely positive. In her view it can easily lead to selfishness and insensitivity: you will do anything to reach your goal even if you have to trample on other people's feelings along the way. That is why her job as a teacher suited her so well. Being a teacher can hardly be called a career as only very few can become school managers, and that was certainly not something she wished to be. Teachers are all promoted after a certain number of years, so there were no grounds for competition. Of course teaching is not without its goals. Her goals had not been for herself but for the children and the results could be seen at the final examinations. But, in her opinion, examinations were not always fair. The best marks were not always given to the most studious and likeable pupils. What you try to give the pupils as far as personal values are concerned is much more difficult to measure and you seldom see the results. After her retirement Inga had had the great pleasure of having visits

Inga in a thoughtful mood

from old pupils and then she understood what their schooldays meant to them.

Her new experience was that a goal can also be something you give yourself without having to involve others. It is something that can give you great satisfaction when you finally reach it, and it can help you getting rid of stress, as it turned out in her case.

The C5 had a positive effect within a very short space of time.

4.3 C5 Practicing

At the same time as Inga started clearing out her house she began practicing the C5 concept that I taught her. Inga does the exercises in the morning before she starts her other daily activities. The best thing is to practice outside, but as it is often rather cold and windy, she practices in front of an open door. The first exercise is a kind of prayer. To whom you address it is up to each individual. As Inga had never prayed before, she found it a little strange at first. She believes that there is a power stronger than ourselves somewhere and the thought of leaving your worries to that power attracted her. Praying to that power for help to solve some of her problems was not so strange a thought after all. And once Inga had started praying, it became a natural thing and at the same time it gave her some sort of relief. She prayed for help to clear up her house, for help to make her a better human being, less selfish and egoistic, help for understanding her fellow beings better under the motto "Nothing too big, nothing too small". Inga had heard an old beautiful prayer of uncertain origin through a friend who passed away some years ago. It is known as the Serenity Prayer and is attributed to Reinhold Niebuhr, an American protestant theologian. Others say it is older and perhaps written by the famous Italian Saint Francesco from Assisi. It sounds like this:

Grant me the serenity
To accept the things I cannot change,
The courage to change the things I can,
And the wisdom to see the difference

And if you could achieve this, you would certainly be a calmer and wiser person, she thought.

After about five minutes of prayer she goes on to a breathing exercise.

I told Inga to breathe in slowly while counting to five (not aloud but in her head) and hold her breath while she counted to five again, then breathe out. Then she is to repeat this for ten minutes, taking care that the air goes all the way down to the stomach and does not stop in the chest. It is an exercise you can do many times a day. Sometimes Inga even practices it in the bus, when she is going to town. These exercises developed a feeling of calmness and balance in her.

The last exercise Inga does is a concentration exercise which she practices for 15 minutes. I asked her to close her eyes and think of a thing that she likes, and she was to picture this in front of her inner eyes and shut out all thoughts that came to her mind. She pictured a beautiful rose, but especially in the beginning it was very difficult to stop other thoughts popping up in her mind. It is easier now after half a year of practice, but Inga can still be disturbed in her concentration, especially in periods where many things are going on in her life. But you have to be patient and it is a good exercise that gives you calm and peace of mind.

Before she goes to sleep at night she goes through all the things she has experienced during the day, trying to think what effect these events have had on her mind, what positive and negative feelings they gave her and why. Very often she falls asleep before she has gone through all her day!

Inga says, "I can honestly say that I have changed after these eight months. I feel that I have become happier, more observant, a better listener, calmer, and this has allowed me to sleep better, so if you can achieve all this after less than a year, I can see no reason why I should not continue, and I look forward to doing so."

4.4 Impact factor

Living in our industrial world under the bombardment of lots of impressions every hour of the day is a stress factor for our bodies and minds. Some people are better at tackling this than others, but no matter how strong your body and mind are, the daily stress factors will surely affect you and your surroundings.

Stress is contagious. If you are stressed because your daily life is too busy, it will affect your family life and your life with friends and colleagues. Your threshold will be low and you will easily get irritated. In general you are well aware of yourself and a bad conscience is often its side effect. After some time your body will start telling you that something is

Inga is in full concentration

wrong and if you go to your doctor, he will probably tell you that your blood pressure is too high and give you medicine for that. This will remove the symptoms but not the cause.

Many people start going to fitness centers because they know that it is important to be in good physical condition. But what they do not realize is that body and mind are inseparable, and nursing the mind should be just as natural as nursing the body.

It is generally accepted that stress damages centers in your brain, centers that are connected to memory and concentration and learning abilities. Breathing exercises have a beneficial effect on stress.

So it seems that there is a great need for giving people simple tools to improve their concentration and to give them more energy and calmness.

The answer is exercises that require no special place, just a private room where you can practice no matter the time of day.

It is not difficult to imagine what effect this would have on people's life and their communication with each other. If you can work in an atmosphere of calmness and contentment this positive energy will spread like rings affecting each other in the water.

The illustration shows the impact of C5 spreading from one person to another just like circular rings spreading in water.

Inga feels now there have been new developments, especially concerning meditation. She finds it easier to reach a state of mind where she can let her thoughts wander without control and where she is totally relaxed. When the alarm clock sounds after 15 minutes she really feels that she has been away in another world. After 'coming back' there is a period of time where she finds that she is able to concentrate much more on what she is doing, and she sees things more clearly than before. It is a state of mind that can last for a couple of hours, and then it vanishes again.

Doing her daily exercises is no longer something she sees as a duty but something she looks forward to do. Of course there are still days where she feels less concentrated, but they are rarer now. She is looking forward to starting her second phase of exercises. She thinks that it is important not to rush into it and that the more time is spent on each phase, the better the impact will be. You have to have a total grasp of one phase before you move on to the next.

Right: Rings in the wat
(Photo: colourbox.com

Chapter 5

Toward Quality of Life (QoL)

Life is short and it has a definite end. So, it should be full of happiness and pleasure. Every moment should be fully utilized for creating a wonderful Quality of Life (QoL).

Stress-free, tension-free and nights of deep sleep are three measurement parameters of a person's QoL. So, the question is how to make a wonderful Quality of Life?

C5 is the foundation of QoL. Therefore, to have a wonderful QoL, you should build a strong foundation.

The figure illustrates a wonderful Quality of Life, as a result of a strong foundation in C5.

'A positive environment creates "genius" in the world. Genius is sometimes hidden and it has to be brought out by a proper environment'

5.1 Quality of Life (QoL)

We live in a materialistic age. A good Quality of Life is said to be when you have a challenging job, wealth, luxury and all modern facilities including wireless gadgets. But the non-materialistic aspects of life are also important nowadays. Materialism can fill your life with stress and life becomes meaningless if you are always under a heavy workload and suffer from stress, tension, and sleepless nights.

Stressful life

Although the person in the illustration lives in luxury and wealth, she is always stressed, tense and does not get enough sleep. Is this a good Quality of Life? No, it is not. Managing stress needs a clear understanding of your mental state. You need to understand how to unlock your hidden mental potential. You should always remember that there is more strength in a person than you have ever realized or even imagined. It is likely that those who do not believe they have such great strength of mind do so because they have not discovered it or used it. Like many things in life, the mind atrophies in an intellectual sense with lack of use. The potential will never be realized so long as its existence is never known. You do not realize the potential of your mind but further you lock it in even more by stress, tension and lack of sleep to create a big mental block. A locked mind cannot generate creative and innovative idea but leads to locked personalization.

The C5 concept provides a series of steps that will help you 'unlock' your mind. C5 provides a foundation on which to build a life full of creativity that leads to success with no stress, no tension and peaceful sleep at night; in other words it can help provide you with a genuine Quality of Life (QoL). You just have to spend a very small part of the 24 hours of the day: 15 to 60 minutes depending on what is available. This is all you have to spend daily to achieve a good QoL. It helps a person to always be in a pleasant mood and to enjoy a sound sleep at night. If you achieve this QoL, you will automatically unlock your personalization.

The simple conclusion is that C5 will automatically lead to a good Quality of Life for everyone who opens the wide door to achieve the goal of personalization. As shown, it will make you full of happiness.

What does a person need to do?

> **People come and go.
> Between the two,
> C5 plays!!
> C5 only
> needs
> a small
> percentage
> of your time!**

It is a good saying and it needs to be practiced every day.

5.2 Making C5 happen

Chapters 1-4 and Section 5.1 have explained the role and value of C5 in creating a good QoL and thus unlocking your personalization. It is a proven fact that C5 is the foundation for a happy QoL. Therefore it is a must for everyone to make C5 happen in their daily lives. Section 2.8 describes how to practice C5. In the beginning it looks as if C5 can make everything possible in terms of good QoL. The fact is that C5 stimulates creative thinking, promotes contentment, builds up confidence, brings calmness, and all this happens as a result of concentration. Concentration, concentration, concentration, concentration and concentration is the real C5. Concentration brings you into the meditation phase and thus you get the strength to focus on achieving the goal of personalization.

As discussed in Section 2.8 there are various phases in C5. In phase 1, you learn the principle of C5 and start practicing it. You meet several problems in the concentration exercises. After some time you are able to concentrate uninterrupted for a few minutes, perhaps up to five minutes. This gives you a unique experience.

As shown, in the first phase a person practicing C5 finds it difficult to chase away stray thoughts. She hardly manages to concentrate for more than a few seconds in the beginning. But, slowly it gets better and better. The person in the illustration is concentrating on a rose flower.

In fact you need a lot of patience to continue practicing C5 in phase 1. But once you have started, it becomes a routine in your daily life. This is the toughest problem in crossing to phase 2 of C5. With patience, everyone is able complete it successfully.

Phase 2 is a very fascinating phase. If you complete it, you will be able to concentrate for more than fifteen minutes, a really remarkable achievement. The results are unimaginable.

A person in phase 2 is illustrated in the second image. In a step-by-step process you increase your concentration

span from five to ten minutes, and then to 15 minutes. Great pleasure and calmness is the result.

After phase 2, you move very fast. Within a year's time, you are able to concentrate for more than 30 minutes. Reaching the goal of one hour is quite tough, but it is definitely achievable. After that, the sky is the limit. Phase 3 is depicted in the third figure. This phase brings you into the ultimate reality. The images clearly show the differences between the three phases.

5.3 A dream toward reality and truth

It is always good to dream about the future. But then you should put an effort into making the dream a reality and a truth. This book is an example of making a dream reality and a truth.

Chapters 1 and 2 discuss the C5 principles and program. C5 represents my dream. Chapter 3 presents a case study based on the facts and experiences of Leo, which effectively show that C5 is a reality. In Chapter 4, Inga's decision to practice C5 is discussed. Her experience shows that C5 is not only a reality but a truth. So my dream is brought into reality and truth by Leo and Inga.

After reaching this phase, I realized that the door to C5 should be opened to everyone. A third person has already gone ahead and is practicing, and a couple are slowly getting started.

As I write, there is no literature on C5. This is the first book about the concept. In due course other books will follow. Since it is meant as an introduction to C5, it was decided to make it short so that anybody can read it. To gain detailed knowledge you will have to read the books to come.

My mind holds the full picture of what C5 is about. The task is to train other people and by means of a chain reaction, it will spread all over the globe.

This is the way of every new, unique invention. At the age of 16 (in 1962) I invented C5. From the age of 16 to 56, I had the opportunity to train several people and also to practice myself. When I was 56 (in 2002) Leo and I started talking about C5, and I was 62 (in 2008) when Inga expressed her interest in practicing C5. The first C5 book will be published when I am at the age of 65, and many more things will happen when I am at the age of 66 (in 2012) and beyond.

In order to make the work effective and of service to humankind, a basic mind-body center will be launched to educate and train people. The Center for Human Mind and Body (CHMB) is discussed in the following section.

5.4 Unlocking the personalization

The ideas of C5 will be further developed in a global Center for Human Mind and Body (CHMB) based on an inter-/cross-disciplinary concept with focus on human innovation. The key goals of the activities will be efficiency, quality and punctuality. The C5 concept will effect a paradigm shift in innovative research and higher education in the area of emerging human mind-body philosophy and psychology. The vision of C5 is to become

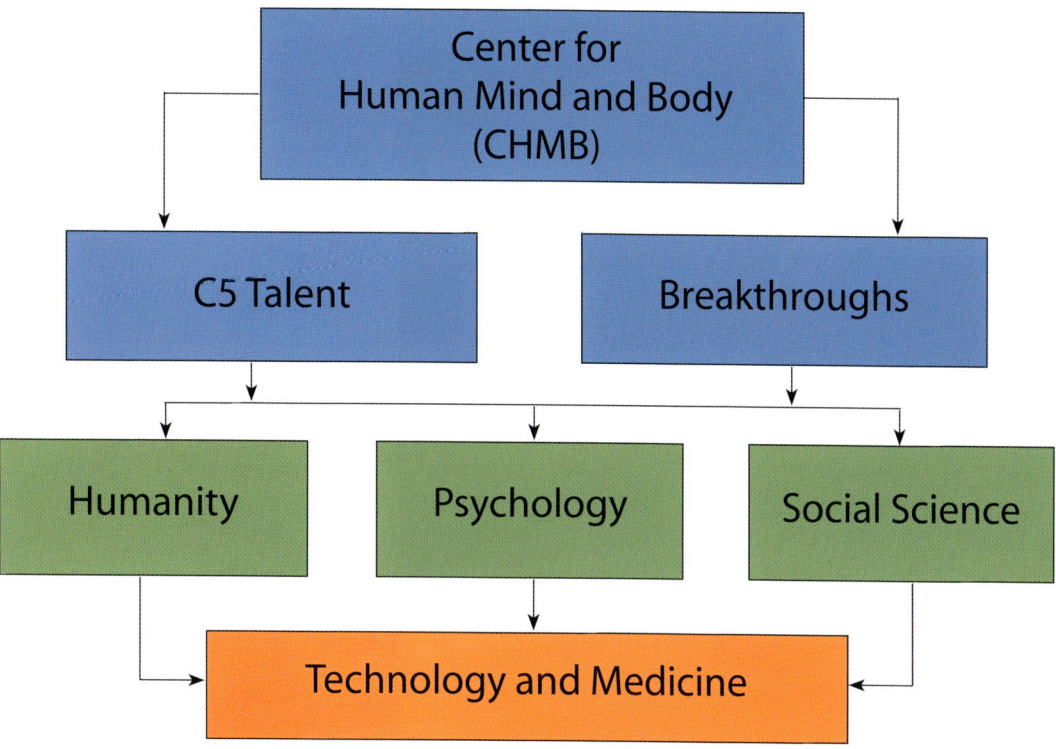

The C5 concept and Center for Human Mind and Body (CHMB)

a globally recognized center for research on mind and body to improve the quality of life (QoL). The concept, which allows for a full integration of my vision on C5, is illustrated in the figure.

The direct results of work at CHMB are represented by the blocks 'C5 Talent' and 'Breakthroughs'. C5 practitioners at the center will conduct exploratory studies for the achievement of groundbreaking innovations. Their fundamental research for the development of C5 expertise will be reflected in the growth of the universal Quality of Life (QoL). With time, the results will lead to revolutionary advances toward the unlocking of the personalization.

Author
Ramjee Prasad

Professor Ramjee Prasad is currently Director of Center for TeleInFrastruktur (CTIF) and holds the chair of Wireless Information and Multimedia Communications at Aalborg University, Denmark. He has published over a thousand technical papers, contributed to several books, and has authored, co-authored, or edited more than 25 books. *Unlock Your Personalization* is the most recent. He is the inventor of several new ideas, among which he considers the C5 concept as the most precious.

Ramjee Prasad was born on July 1, 1946 in Babnaur (Gaya), India, near Bodh Gaya, which is famous as the place where Gautama Buddha attained Enlightenment under the Bodhi tree. Bodh Gaya has been a constant inspiration and a source of positive energy throughout his life. Professor Prasad conceived the C5 concept in July 1962 when he was 16 years old. In India he gave lessons in C5 to many prominent figures from the legal field such as lawyers and judges. C5 is the source of his happy family life as well as his scientific achievements. He was inspired to present the C5 concept to a broader audience on seeing the successful results achieved by his two pupils and friends, Leo and Inga.

Unlock Your Personalization
By Ramjee Prasad

© The author and Aalborg University Press, 2012

Layout by akila / Kirsten Bach Larsen

Photos by Adam Lehn, Rajeev Prasad, Leo Ligthart, Vrinda H. Kurande and Colourbox
All paintings are property of Aalborg University, Denmark

Language editing by Morten Berg

Printed at Toptryk Grafisk ApS, Denmark, 2012

ISBN 978-87-7112-028-8

Published by
Aalborg University Press
Skjernvej 4A, 2nd floor
DK - 9220 Aalborg
Phone +45 99407141
E-mail aauf@forlag.aau.dk
www.forlag.aau.dk

All rights reserved. No part of this book may be reprinted or reproduced or utilized in any form or by any electronic, mechanical, or other means, now known or hereafter invented, including photocopying and recording, or in any information storage or retrieval system, without permission in writing from the publishers, except for reviews and short excerpts in scholarly publications.